Rev. George R. Hunsberger, Ph.D., Professor of Missiology and Director of the Doctor of Ministry Program, Western Theological Seminary, Holland, Michigan USA:

This book tells the compelling story of the deep roots from which Liberia International Christian College has arisen through one man's lifelong hunger for education and his passionate desire to help his country establish a sustainable future. In the course of the story, African and American cultures find themselves in conversation, sometimes tugging at each other, sometimes joining forces. In the end, each plays a role in forming the wide foundations necessary to begin what some believe is "the first indigenous college in Liberia."

The long story of Sei's own life and educational path shows the considerable roots from which the LICC vision and plan have come. This shared vision developed in Sei's companions, in people who come alongside to assist him throughout his education and ministry, and among fellow Liberians who now live in America but have refused to forget their homeland.

What makes this book wonderful is the way one small boy's emerging story, a story of God's intentions for the world and a story of a nation's struggle toward a better future, are woven together.

I would add that as a student in my courses in the 1990s, Sei exhibited the desire for learning which the book describes!

Dave Rodriguez, Senior Pastor, Grace Community Church, Noblesville, Indiana:

I am overwhelmed by the scope of the journey Sei and Yah have been on. This book offers true stories of trusting God in the middle of chaos and an undetermined future. It helps clearly define hope and faith. Very few people have ever or will ever share the breadth of journey the Buors have had. It is simply amazing how God has directed them!

Dr. Gordon J. Van Wylen, President Emeritus, Hope College, Holland, Michigan:

This book is a fine testimony of how God reached into Sei's life and then impacted the Church and the nation of Liberia through his life. Readers will learn about the background of the country of Liberia, the tragic Civil War there, and what God is doing today in Liberia.

Herb Jacobsen, Ph.D., Chair of the Board, Jerusalem University College, Former Professor of Theology at Wheaton College:

I have known Sei for many years. Throughout all that time, I have witnessed his unwavering love for Liberia and its people, his desire to address the educational needs of his homeland, and his vision for a new and better Liberia. This story is profoundly inspirational.

Ray Hilbert, CEO / Co-Founder Truth@work, Co –Author The Janitor and The Carrot Chaser:

I was amazed and humbled to read all that Sei has been through: the challenges, the loss of family, friends, and loved ones throughout his war-torn nation, and the difficulties of achieving his educational and personal goals. But more so, I am amazed and you will be also, at the power of God's faithfulness in the life of a faithful man.

Joe Williamson, tSOAR Ministries and Senior Vice President - Investments, Wells Fargo Advisors:

From the opening of Sei's story, one can see God planting the seeds of what He ultimately called Sei to do. Over the years, the theme of education wove through his life as well as God's provision of all he needed to transform this simple Liberian tribesman into a leader for educational and spiritual transformation in Liberia.

NO MORE WAR:
Rebuilding Liberia through Faith, Determination and Education

Dr. Sei Buor

iUniverse, Inc.
New York   Bloomington

NO MORE WAR:

Rebuilding Liberia through Faith, Determination and Education

iUniverse books may be ordered through booksellers or by contacting:

iUniverse
1663 Liberty Drive
Bloomington, IN 47403
www.iuniverse.com
1-800-Authors (1-800-288-4677)

ISBN: 978-1-4401-5655-7 (sc)
ISBN: 978-1-4401-5654-0 (ebook)

Printed in the United States of America

iUniverse rev. date: 9/30/2009

NO MORE WAR:
Rebuilding Liberia through Faith,

Determination and Education

Dr. Sei Buor

Dedicated in the memory
of
Eugenie Therese Lee De Haas of Orono, Maine
Jan. 22, 1927 – March 26, 2007
She was my first international vision partner (since 1986) and
was called to heaven before the vision became a reality.

and

Dr. Herman De Haas, who continues to support
the vision after the passing of Eugenie.

Herman, Yah, Sei, and Eugenie in 2001

and
My father, Chief Buor, who first invested in my
early education, equipping and empowering me to
give back to my community and nation.

and

The children of Liberia who for decades have longed for a college education that is affordable and accessible.

and

The courageous ULICAF men and women who, despite their struggles as refugees in America, surrender to God and give their all – resources, talents, time – to create the Liberia International Christian College.

NO MORE WAR:
Rebuilding Liberia through Faith, Determination and Education

Foreword
By Bill Ellison

My interest in the life and vision of Dr. Sei Buor and the work he is doing began long before the events cited in this book. For me it started as a kid. I would hear on the news or read in the paper, amidst the usual stories about sports teams, weather, local interest tidbits, etc, that 250,000 people were killed by a monsoon in Bangladesh or that 200,000 people died in a famine in Ethiopia. These items seemed to be noted by the media in passing, as if they were everyday news. It was later, in early adulthood, that I learned that poverty and loss were not just an occasional disaster but an ongoing and everyday reality for all too many.

When I finished college, I started my engineering career and began to live the life of a middle-class American. Still, I couldn't help but ask, "Why was I born into relative prosperity in the U.S., instead of into a far more desperate situation in the third-world?" Eventually, as I considered this fortunate and unearned grace, I felt motivated to give to those in need. I participated in various relief organizations and ministries whose goal was to alleviate misery and poverty. I comfortably thought I was doing some good.

Even if temporary, my giving did produce results. The various relief organizations and ministries did mitigate the effects of some natural disaster or enable many to live another day. However, as the decades slipped by, I noticed that the extraordinary needs continued – and continued, and sometimes even got worse.

I expressed my frustration to an East-African educational leader from Kenya. His immediate response was, "Ah, but you've got to love Africa!" and, "Yes, 'donor fatigue' is a problem." I related to the donor fatigue part, but the part about loving Africa I wasn't too sure about. I was beginning to realize my actions were more borne out of obedience and generalized compassion than a personal love for those in need.

That realization changed my life and my giving. In our day of jet travel and Internet connectivity, that question asked of Jesus, "And who is my neighbor?" … might today just as easily be answered by the question, "Who is not my neighbor?" I resolved to get more personally involved in the lives of those I was trying to help.

It helped that I had a close friend who was spending his retirement years, and social security check, feeding kids in the foothills of Mt. Kilimanjaro, Tanzania. He had even sent several kids on to trade school or University. Through that friend, I began to participate in the lives of individuals, and now really saw them as brothers and sisters. Eventually, I was able to spend a month in East Africa and found my focus in helping with the education of students. I also began to realize the efficacy of small micro-finance projects. Via such initiatives, I hoped to provide – for at least a few Africans – the chance to change their life circumstances, and those of their families.

But, I still had the lingering questions, "What are the root causes of such difficult circumstances?" or, "How do we arrive at sustainable change that truly makes a difference for Africa?" I can't say I had answers to such questions, but I was open to them.

I got to know Sei through a Saturday morning Bible Study. When I first heard Sei's story, I was captivated. The more I heard, the more captivated I became. As a white, urban professional, growing up and even now living in Indianapolis, I never experienced those types of trials or dangers. Though some might say that his life is a fascinating adventure filled with excitement, tragedy, redemption, pain and joy – and indeed it is all of that – it is even a more incredible story of grace – God's Grace in leading a small boy into faith in Him and into a life of education which has yielded perspective, understanding, and a vision beyond seeking his own individual prosperity.

More than being moved by his story, I was moved by his vision. With his countrymen, Dr. Sei Buor is creating an institution (Liberian International Christian College) that will help develop Godly leaders. Sei is focusing on changing the fundamentals – addressing the root causes of problems leading to poverty, strife, and civil war. He is focused on helping make Liberia (and West Africa) better in the longer-term. From the terrible experience of having seen his family and country destroyed by a civil war, and from the depths of a loving heart for his Lord and Master, Jesus Christ, my friend Sei has been faithful to the vision in creating this school. He is working so that next generations of Liberians and Africans might have the opportunity to address root causes of difficult issues, gain skills and an education – and emerge with prosperous lives.

And change must begin at the root cause of all issues – the human heart. If the heart is redeemed, life circumstances will follow. But, awareness, changed hearts, and societal redemption all result from information (faith is believing some things about some One, and "how shall they hear without a preacher?") and further education. Faith education, skills and knowledge education, and wisdom (gleaned from knowledge and awareness), and material assistance are all needed to draw people out of dollar-per-day subsistence living which is characteristic of much of the world.

Sei Buor is a living manifestation of that process. Sei pursued education, but his life was changed forever by the greatest Teacher of all – Jesus Christ. Sei has clearly understood that the Lord has blessed him so that he can be a greater blessing to others. He has used his education and skills to start working towards building up his community. It was not often an easy path, but those trials have developed a depth of character and wisdom.

As you will see as you read his story, his vision, character, and commitment have been honed by many challenging circumstances and trials of faith. That character, and his vision, is the reason I encouraged him to capture and share his story in writing. I believe you too will be moved by Sei's story. As you read this book, please consider how God is using you to impact the world. If you find that addressing root causes and training new leaders for Africa is something you want to see happening, please consider supporting Liberian International Christian College.

Acknowledgements

I never imagined what God would do through me, much less that I would earn a doctorate of philosophy in America, then found a college in my native Liberia, and now write a book about my journey. However, during all of these years, remarkable individuals have given special meaning to my life, opened their hearts and doors to me, supported me and believed in me. Without such personal support, the college and this book would not have been possible.

I have been overwhelmed by the generosity demonstrated to me by the people named below, who offered their time and knowledge and who inspired me by sharing their successes as well as their frustrations in life. You will see many of their names and stories within the book; some have preferred to play a more "behind the scenes role." My deepest thanks to all of them for their contributions, and for keeping me going during the many months of pulling this book together. My immense gratitude goes to my family - my wife, Yah and our five lovely children, Olivia, Lily, Tonzia, Deizie and Ben. I am indebted to them for their love and emotional support, which contributed so much towards making the time committed to this project to be a joy, and to making this book become a reality.

Thanks to two special friends and editors, Bill Ellison and Mark Oehler, who prodded me to actually write the book I had talked about for so long, and who nudged me towards its completion. They helped me focus untamed ideas into a sequence of chapters that eventually flowed together to make a story. They diligently read and re-read my many drafts and offered critical comments, which not only assisted me to produce a refined manuscript but also helped make me a more skillful writer in the process.

Thanks to several friends who also read, critiqued, and made invaluable comments on the early final drafts of this manuscript. They are Dr. Gordon and Margaret Van Wylen, Professor Wayne Weld, John Lieberman, Dr. Peter Nehsahn, and Betty Van Campen.

Thanks especially to all my band of brothers in my Monday morning senior Bible study at Grace Community Church, under the leadership of Mr. Rob Tresso and Gene Shaffer; my Friday morning Bible study also at Grace, under the leadership of John Lieberman and Jay Chambers; our tSOAR discipleship group on Saturday morning at Northview Christian, under the leadership of Joe Williamson; and our small home group, under the leadership of Art and Lynette Small. The influence of all of these people is strong in the pages of this book, and their lives and words continue to teach and inspire me.

I am also very grateful to our ULICAF Board President Karney Dunah, and his beloved wife Lydia. As with Aaron being assigned to Moses, so has God assigned Karney to lead our board, to speak the truth (at board meetings, and in my life as well) and to build relationships within our organization. Karney, your faithfulness to God and to ULICAF is strong indeed!

Special thanks to the empowering ministry of Truth@work under the leadership of Perry Hines and Ray Hilbert. Ray funded my two-year effort to study with other non-profit organizations, so that I would become a more competent and skillful leader for our United Liberian Inland Church and Friends organization.

Finally, when I completed the manuscript for the book, I submitted it to Sally Rushmore to edit for grammar and spelling. She was compelled to read the story from start to finish in a single sitting. In doing so, she realized that some chapters had wonderful storytelling while others were mainly facts. She was sure that what God wanted her to do was to help me tell the story in my voice – in such a way as to pull the reader through the book. As we talked, we began to see that many of the people in the story were still in my life and – through interviews or e-mails – could add their perspective to my story in ways that authenticated and strengthened it.

Introduction:
From My Education to the Education of Liberia

The phone rang again. I looked at the clock; it was 4:00 a.m. The timing was early for me here in America, but back in Liberia, it was already mid-morning. I hesitated. Yes, I was expecting this phone call, but there already had been so many trials, so many obstacles, and so many challenges. This phone call could be the good news we hoped for, the good news we expected. Or, perhaps more realistically, it could be just another challenge that we must prayerfully overcome. I prayed briefly, and then, finally and somewhat reluctantly, I picked up the phone.

It was good news. I nearly jumped with joy! We had received our credentials from the Liberian government! This was a major step. We were now an official school. With these credentials, Liberia International Christian College (LICC) would be able to open its doors. When they graduated, our students would have an accredited government-approved degree. Finally, after so many years, our plans were coming to fruition.

God is good! In the midst of the trouble, it does not always feel that way. But, if we have faith, if we wait on the Lord, if we keep looking for His direction, if we follow His direction as we find it, in the end His plan works out. And, so far, so it has been with us.

Education is important to me. So perhaps it is no surprise that I became a member of a group of Liberian refugees inspired to establish a college in their homeland. We are men and women who were driven from our country by a violent and destructive civil war, and have struggled to earn a living in America. Some of us have worked, or are working, two or three jobs to make ends meet. In the midst of our own struggles, we began looking for a way to help our country. As we met and talked, the idea of a college began to form. It would not be just an ordinary college. It was to be a special school of higher learning where future leaders, godly leaders, would be trained. We would educate men and women who would stand among those who would shape the future of Liberia. These men and women would teach others about God. Hopefully, they would also keep our country from falling into another civil war.

Now, through LICC, we have the chance to help others impact the lives of even more people. By working together, and with the help of many caring Americans, we have been able to found a school.

I had long imagined what it would be like for those first students. It has been one of the things that has kept me going through all the challenges. Many dedicated believers made great sacrifices laying the groundwork to attend college. Sadly, most of these men and women experienced civil war first hand. Even worse, some may have participated in that war and may have fought their countrymen with AK-47s. Many of them have experienced extreme poverty. In spite of these obstacles, they never gave up the hope that one day they would get a college education.

Those students long for the transformation that education can provide. They long for training that will transform their lives from agents of destruction to nation builders. Together, they will be able to restore what Liberia lost during those brutal years of civil war. They will become people who know and live justice.

When I think of those first students, I can't help but think of my own early education. To attend my first school, I had to walk five miles each way. I did so without shoes. I did not feel sorry for myself – no, not at all. None of the other students I walked with had shoes either! I faced the long walk and many other challenges joyfully, because I was thankful for the opportunity to get an education. I believed an education would allow me to help myself, my family, my village, and my country.

But, in the end, I found that education alone was meaningless and left me feeling empty. Ultimately, it was through a relationship with Christ that I found true fulfillment. I discovered this had been part of God's plan too. He used all of my prior experiences and hardships to teach others about Him.

My journey has been a long one. Part of that journey is a story about the value of education. Another part of that journey is a story of the people who helped me along the way. It is a story of opportunities and risks, of challenges and disappointments, of surprises and joys. And, it is also the story of those who I have had the privilege of helping. My entire journey is a story about God.

During my childhood as a young boy back in Riverview, Liberia, I was fascinated by each new thing I learned about life and craved for more education. I did not know where such an aspiration would take me or what the future held for me. I never dreamed that God could one day use me to help build a college and provide educational opportunities for my people.

Please join me as I share some of the joys and heartaches of my journey.

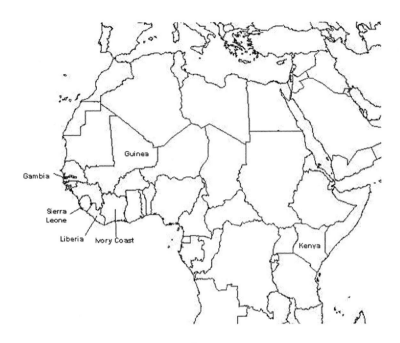

Africa

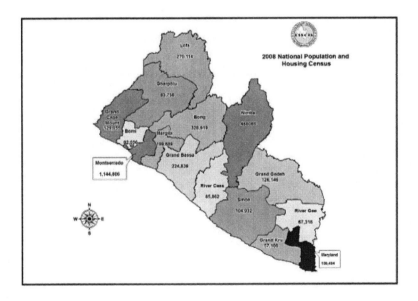

Nimba

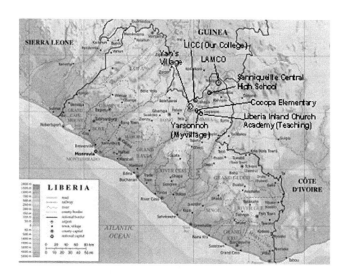

Liberia

This map is licensed under the Creative Commons Attribution ShareAlike 3.0, Attribution ShareAlike 2.5, Attribution ShareAlike 2.0 and Attribution ShareAlike 1.0 License. In short: you are free to share and make derivative works of the file under the conditions that you appropriately attribute it, and that you distribute it only under a license identical to this one http://en.wikipedia.org/wiki/File:Topographic_map_of_Liberia-en.svg

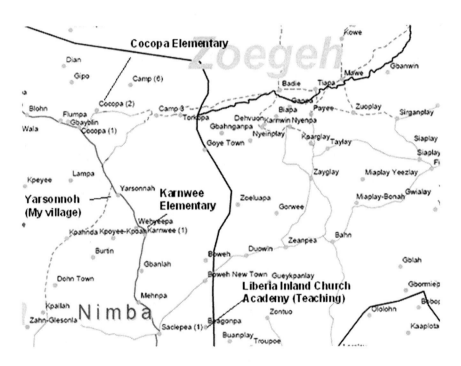

Nimba County

Part I   *Starting the Education Process*

Chapter 1   The Desire for Education Starts

I was born on February 16, 1958 in Yarsonnoh, Nimba County, Liberia. I actually did not know my birthday until I was ten years old. At that time my father's senior wife carefully calculated my birthday by tracing the events surrounding my birth.

The birth of a male or a female child is equally accompanied by celebration and joyful songs; however, among the Mano (my ethnic group or tribe) the birth of a male child takes pre-imminence over that of a girl. First of all, a boy is considered to be an arrow in the hands of his father as well as the clan into which he is born. Secondly, he is the preserver of the family name and legacy. So it was with great expectations that my birth was declared to the outside world with shouts of joy. My clan (immediate family and relatives) gave me the name "Sei," which means "the first fruit of the womb."

My father and mother were subsistence farmers. My father was affectionately called "Chief Buor" in the town of Riverview where he served as a chief for several years. He was well respected and admired by his peers because of his friendliness, hospitality, and generosity.

When my mother (Mama Seayee) was three years old, she and my maternal grandmother (Lekulah) and my aunt (Paylia), entered my father's clan (Lessonoh) as refugees because of intertribal fighting. Upon arrival, they were received and accepted by chief Larway of Yarsonnoh. My grandmother later married chief Larway, who became a stepfather to my mother and her sister.

My father had six wives altogether. His very first wife died when I was about five years old, leaving a boy and a girl. That boy (Big Saye) became one of my closest stepbrothers in the family. He told me years later that he had dreamed of becoming a truck driver. He had left the village to live with a family in the city of Ganta with the hope of obtaining his training through an apprenticeship, but then received the news about his mother's illness and returned to the village, only to learn that his mother's condition had deteriorated. She died shortly thereafter, leaving them in a state of shock and painful grieving. He remained to care for his younger sister and never went back to fulfill his dream of becoming a truck driver.

Looking back on it, I sometimes have wondered what the difference was between him and myself. We both had dreams. His dream never came true. Eventually, mine did. As I've thought about it, I have come to this conclusion: I had both human and supernatural help in achieving my dream. Indeed, one of those helpers was my stepbrother. He took me into his home and provided support for me to go to school. He loved me as the younger brother I was. In my stepbrother's case, he did not have the same type of support. He had set out to do something, but was unable to accomplish it. He, however, never let his life be overcome with bitterness. Maybe he couldn't follow his dream, but he wanted someone else's dream to come true. Then, later in my life, when I became a Christian, I received another type of help: assistance in the spiritual dimension from trusting in God. My stepbrother is still alive today and he is a Christian. But, in those days, he wasn't a Christian. So, by comparison, he didn't have as much human help, nor did he have any spiritual help. This is hindsight and my own evaluation of how God worked in my life over a period of many years. At the time, both my stepbrother and I did the best we could with what we had.

*   *   *   *   *   *   *   *   *   *   *   *

After the death of my father's first wife, his second wife, Yah Quoigbini, took the place of the head-wife. She was given a three-bedroom house. This was done to give her privacy and plenty of rooms to accommodate the children as well as visitors. The other women lived separately under a single roof with a room allocated to each of them. In our culture, a head-wife played the role of a supervisor to all the other wives and was also a "mother" to all the children born into this family. Her responsibilities included mentoring the younger wives and acting as an intermediary between my father and the other wives. Her duties frequently included seeking forgiveness on their behalf when they offended my father and were in danger of physical punishment. She also intervened on behalf of young wives outside of the house, and many times some of them would approach her later to express their gratitude and appreciation for saving them from physical abuse. Unfortunately, this practice was a common form of punishment for the offenses a wife knowingly or unknowing committed.

Yah Quoigbini, whom we called Grandma, as a midwife, personally delivered all of the children born to these women, and she gave personal names to many of them. She was also the family doctor, and became the expert in diagnosing almost all the common illness that plagued the children in the house. She also treated all of these common illnesses with simple herbs from varied trees in the bush; amazingly many of them recovered their health almost instantly. In the case of others, she would advise the mother to take the child to the government health center or missionary clinic. (The health centers were anywhere from seven to fifteen miles and they were reached by walking!) The head-wife was in reality the "manager" of the entire household, including all the other wives and their children.

Beyond her own home, she also played the role of a traditional midwife in the village. She was part of the team of senior ladies who delivered almost all the babies in the village, except for the occasional complicated cases that were referred to the modern health centers. The older men sought her opinions on difficult home making decisions as well as numerous health related issues. She also was a committed peacemaker, and intervened on behalf of the children to prevent them from receiving spankings by my father or their own mothers. Altogether, there were 17 children from the same father and six mothers. Today, there are only nine of us still alive.

My mother (who became known as Rebecca after becoming a Christian) and another lady were the youngest of the wives. The other lady returned to her family after she gave birth to her first son, leaving him in my mother's care. Rebecca had many children of her own as well as a stepson, so a child was always being added to the family. Therefore, my father allocated two rooms to her, one to be used as a bedroom and the other as a kitchen. The older children slept in the kitchen and the younger children slept with her in her bedroom.

Even though my father had so many children, I became very close to my father. When I was very young, he only came to our house occasionally. He had many wives to oversee and it was quite difficult for me to see him and get a chance to talk with him. Once I grew up and was "initiated" into our society, things began to change. In the traditional sense, as boys grew into adulthood, they spent more time with their fathers and less time with their mothers. Later, my father invested in my education. He also inspired me and made me feel that anything I committed myself to I could accomplish. In traditional African society the blessing comes from the father. This can be compared to the time in the Bible when Isaac blessed his two sons. Our tribal traditions hold the belief that a father can still bless his children from heaven.

I will give one example of how my father expressed his love for me. As I grew up, sometimes I needed to earn money for school and other necessities. I would seek employment with farmers who grew cash crops like sugar cane. The work was very demanding. Sometimes my father would come by in the afternoon and help me do the job. He would do more than just help with the physical labor, which was a blessing by itself. He would talk to me and tell me the most interesting stories about his life. He also encouraged me not to give up on my dreams. He was a huge inspiration and encouragement in my life. He also taught me moral values, emphasizing that I was to never engage in adultery with another man's wife.

I can imagine that the polygamous part of my early family life would sound very strange to Westerners. However, back in those days, it was an accepted part of our culture. That is not to say that all West African men were polygamous or that polygamy doesn't have its problems! But, it is just to say it was not unusual for someone of my generation to grow up, like I did, in a polygamous family.

Some of my ancestors, like my grandmother, had experienced the threat of violence and civil war. However, in my early childhood in Riverview, I had no fear of violence. My childhood was a materially poor by Western standards, but it was a relatively happy one. War and conflict were a long way from us. My world was our village, and our village lived in peace.

*   *   *   *   *   *   *   *   *   *   *   *

Liberia is on the west coast of Africa. The name Liberia denotes "liberty" or "Land of the Free." In 1822, the American Colonization

Society established Liberia as a place to send freed African-American slaves. African-Americans gradually migrated to the colony and became a new ethnic group known as Americo-Liberians, where many present day Liberians trace their ancestry. On July 26, 1847, the Americo-Liberian settlers declared independence for The Republic of Liberia. The Americo-Liberians who had previously established a country among the various tribal groups, with assistance from the Government of the United States, came together to establish a true state – much in the same manner as the Colonies in America came together to form the United States.

The settlers regarded Africa as a "Promised Land," but they did not integrate into traditional African society. Once in Africa, they referred to themselves as "Americans" and were recognized as such by local Africans and by British colonial authorities in neighboring Sierra Leone. The symbols of the new state — its flag, motto, and seal — and the form of government that they chose reflected their American background and their Diaspora experience.

However, as we were to find out later, the introduction of this new ethnic mix compounded ethnic tensions with the sixteen other main ethnicities already existing for centuries. One of those ethnicities was the Mano tribe into which I was born.

*   *   *   *   *   *   *   *   *   *   *   *

The Beginning of My Education

There are two educational systems in Liberia: indigenous and Western. I have studied in both schools. The indigenous education focuses on basic survival skills. Food is a necessity. We had to learn to obtain it and prepare it if we wanted to have something to eat. If we wanted clothing, we had to make our own outfits, and so someone needed to know how to make clothes.

Besides our formal education with other youths, we also learned the shared wisdom and heritage of our specific ethnic group. This training begins almost from the time we first begin to talk. The immediate family was most important, but members of extended families and the entire clan played significant roles in our lives. Among the

Mano people, rearing of the children was seen as the responsibility of all members of the clan. Each tribal member understood that the tribe and its unique identity could only be preserved and extended as long as the emerging generations followed the ways of their elders.

Education was not separate from life; it was vital to life itself. Instruction in cultural and spiritual matters often took the form of storytelling. This is especially true since there was no formal written language in the indigenous tribes. Youths who exhibited a keen memory and storytelling ability might be chosen to become the anointed culture bearers and they, then, would be trained to become the next generation of storytellers.

Like all Mano boys, my indigenous education included our "away from the home" initiation time and male circumcision. I was about six years old when I went through my initiation rites. This initiation gives a boy "the right of passage" from childhood to young adulthood. The educational part of the initiation is called the "Poro."

Every youth must receive this initiation training before he can be considered worthy to assume village responsibilities. The school classroom and instruction were not held in the village or town, but instead in permanent places selected in the forest about fifteen to twenty miles from the town. This special section of the bush was never used for any other purpose, and every district had its own school and special forest preserve for this purpose. The secluded nature of the school gave rise to the label "devil bush or "bush school" by non-members. It is really not known when the Poro began or how it emerged, but it is considered one of the oldest educational systems.

Like other youths, I left town to attend this school. The girls went for separate and different training than that for the boys. In the Poro for boys, I was taught both practical and theoretical lessons. As an example of theory, we were taught stories about history, ethics, war, and defense. The practical parts were the physical things that we learned, such as wrestling, fishing, and hunting. We attended for about a year which was the typical duration for the Poro in our area.

In short, this Poro schooling taught us basic life survival skills. We learned to provide for ourselves using what we found alone in nature. I admired the discipline that this taught us. The indigenous schooling helped make us independent young boys ever ready for any challenge and confident to care for ourselves. In America, when most people think about surviving in the wilderness, they think about some back-packing trip. It was not so for us village boys growing up. We might have to live in the jungle with wild animals. We were taught skills there so that we wouldn't have to rely on our mothers to cook for us. We learned how to find food to eat. We were taught to survive without access to Western clothing. If we wanted or needed something, we had to create it. There was also no store or pantry.

For example, when we built a shelter, we had to climb up palm trees, cut leaves, and haul them back to the site we had cleared. We did this as a group. Everyone did what they were able to do. Young children might only fetch water or carry a few leaves. The shelter was built for the community and by the community. Typically, five to ten of us would build a shelter to live in. My job, as I was quite young, was to haul leaves to the spot we had cleared. I also had the assignment to go get water. There was, of course, no running water. If a creek was nearby, we would use it. If there was no creek, we had to dig a well. I did both, depending on what was needed for our camp.

Following the Poro schooling, we went through the circumcision rite, which is the most significant aspect of the initiation process. These experiences and events are never forgotten. Among our Mano and the Kpelle (an allied tribe) the tribal initiations ranged from one to four years. In other tribes, like the Loma and Dei, it could be from two to eight years! The Poro primarily focuses on marital laws, oral history, individual and social deference, communal values, and work and ethics standards.

The head of the Poro School was the Zo (grandmaster). A Zo was proficient in the indigenous codes of law, craft, and history. He was especially renowned for sound discretion. The village chiefs and elders were highly venerated by the younger due to the great prestige of their position. The Poro sought to instill in us the core values of our culture. Individuals were equipped not only to deal successfully with moral and social responsibilities, but also to obtain subsistence from the physical environment. If one was to advance and gain trust and recognition in Mano society, it was mandatory that he successfully complete the Poro.

In our village, the indigenous training for females was called the "Sande." It was also held in seclusion, but it was a lot shorter and less rigid. Before the beginning of the Sande session, the men would surrender the forest to the women to ensure cooperation and respect. Girls were admitted between the ages of four and twelve. Initiation took place in a designated enclosure in the forest about a mile or two from the village. The school trained the girls in those ideals, attitudes, and skills which the culture valued in female adults. The values were respect for the elders and husbands, pride in motherhood, and an ability to work and help support the family.

Incidentally, I did not learn about what happened in the Sande school from my sisters. They were not allowed to tell me! But during my own experience in the Poro, we were given a general description of what happened in the girls' school. Our teachers did not go into detail, because the women's experience, like ours, was considered sacred and was to be kept private and secret.

Like the Poro, the Sande graduation was crowned by a ceremony. Also, like the boys, the girls received new names based on their position and accomplishments in the society. Gifts were given and speeches were made. The supreme grandmaster delivered the primary speech, which was followed by remarks from other leading men and women in the community. For about two months, the graduates visited other adjacent towns and villages and performed traditional dances to demonstrate what they had recently learned. Each graduate pledged her allegiance to the Sande institution.

While the boys were trained in the Poro School in physical combat and mental and decision-making skills, the girls' education in the Sande school focused on the virtues of chastity, morality, and fidelity. The females are expected to be efficient in domestic duties and to take pride in this calling. The girls were well trained in utilizing traditional medicines. This skill was considered the highest form of practical training they could obtain. The initiates also specialized in the arts of singing and dancing. The integrity and preservation of the family was so central to our culture that marital chastity and fidelity was fundamental to moral character development. The instruction emphasized respect for her husband and for all the elderly members of the community. Hospitality was always important. There was also training in food preparation, cooking, and food preservation.

Motherhood was also an important part of the instruction. The girls learned about personal hygiene, acceptable food and drink, and what foods to abstain from during pregnancy. Only graduates of the Sande were eligible to be midwives. Even if professional women were trained in the modern art of midwifery, if they were not from the Sande, they were looked down upon and (in some cases) prohibited from practicing as a midwife. Upon graduation the girls were considered ready for marriage. However, in the case of very young girls, the marriage might not actually be consummated for many years.

In essence, long before the beginnings of Liberian recorded history, my ancestors, the indigenous peoples, developed a system of education that maintained our cultural traditions and social organization, and thus united our society.

Chapter 2   Two Very Different Schools

I learned how to survive in the bush Poro School. I had accepted, as a way of life, subsistence farming. I learned to respect the traditions of my tribe, but I was also fortunate in that my future education would combine traditional African schooling with a Western education. This is because, early in my childhood, I had the chance to attend a western-style school, the Karnwee Elementary School.

My father surprised me one evening by asking me to take a seat by his side. My first thought was that one of the elders had seen me misbehaving somewhere and had secretly reported this to my father. The call, however, was more cordial than expected, especially if my meeting was for an incident of misbehaving. After several minutes of silence, he said that we were waiting for someone to join us. Before long, Harrison Dolo, a young man from the village came in. Upon his arrival, my father explained that the purpose of the meeting was to announce that he was ready for me to begin my Western-style schooling. This young man was to be my facilitator-coach. This would be my first opportunity to enter an actual Western classroom.

Immediately, my father began to outline the responsibilities that Harrison (my guidance boy) would have. He was to take me to the headmaster at Karnwee Elementary School (about 5 to 10 miles away from the village). My father spoke in a manner like he was commanding Harrison. He then gave him a list of responsibilities. Harrison was to serve as my bodyguard to protect me from older boys that often bullied other children that walked the long distance to the school. Harrison was physically well-built and very strong, so he was well-suited for that task. Then, my father commanded Harrison to be my guard/protector against kidnappers.

In those days there were rumors that Americo-Liberians (descendants of freed slaves from America) and their local political allies routinely kidnapped indigenous children for human sacrifices. This act was allegedly done by the "UBF" (United Brothers Fellows) secret society, which was a perverted form of masonry brought over from America.

Harrison accepted every word of instruction from my father. I was eager to get started, but we would have to wait for a couple of weeks before beginning the actual journey. I anxiously waited for the day to arrive. As part of the preparation, my mother bought me a pair of slippers (or flip flops), an exercise notebook with about 12 pages, and a pencil. Very few children had a pair of shoes, but no one actually talked or worried about it.

The night before we finally left, Harrison came by to remind my parents of our early morning departure and to ask for their help in making sure I would wake up and be ready on time. My father reached into in his sack cloth, a traditional pocket book, and pulled out a fifty-cent-piece and handed it to Harrison. He said, "This is your brother's registration fee to be given to the headmaster." This was the school's required registration or tuition fee. Once again, my father went over the instructions in detail, like a specific job description for Harrison: "Hand him over to the headmaster, protect him from bullies, protect him against kidnappers, and also discipline him as required for bad behavior."

In subsequent years, I was to find out that the elementary school was built in the 1960s through President John F. Kennedy education program initiative for Africa. Since the school existed only in a central regional location, we would be walking about 10 miles round trip from our village on a daily basis. This may seem like a long way, but there were other villages even further away that sent their children to the school.

The headmaster, Lawrence Tozo, was known for enforcing strict discipline. Everyone had to be on time; it did not matter how far you had to walk. You had to be on time and be in your line for the morning devotion, which consisted of singing the Liberian national anthem and raising the flag before heading off to classes. The devotion and opening exercises began at 7:30 a.m. and took about an hour. Classes began about 8:30 a.m. and ran until about 3:00 p.m. with a short break at noon.

Promptness was strictly enforced and tardy students were severely dealt with by the headmaster. The punishment ranged from receiving a whipping, to suspension from school, or hard labor around the building while others continued their learning. Every student was obviously quite fearful of arriving at school late. Because of this fear, Harrison and the other boys and I would leave our village very early in the morning to begin the five-mile walk to school. There were about 20 boys on this journey, and the older boys served as bodyguards to the younger ones.

Our village was on the banks of the Yar River and carried the name "Yarsonnoh," which means Riverview or "by the river." We had no electricity, running water, or indoor plumbing. The river was our source for everything, for drinking water, for washing our clothes, and even for bathing. A small creek, "Red Water," named because of its appearance, was on the south side of our village. It joined the Yar River right there in the village. During the rainy season (July to September) both rivers would overflow and literally turn the village into an island.

Since we had to get up so early, there was no time in the morning to take baths. We took our bath in the evening, got our clothes ready, and prepared a little food to take on the journey. There was a small creek near the school where we stopped and washed our feet, faces, and changed into the school uniform before we arrived on campus. The school ran five days a week from February to December with a Christmas break for a little over two months.

Although there were twenty to twenty-five of us from our village who started that school year, only a few made it to the end of the year. Several became sick and dropped out. A whole group might drop out if their guidance boy quit or got sick himself. Others also dropped out because they were late and were severely punished. After such punishment, they might leave and never return. The school or headmaster was not really concerned about those who dropped out since most came from villages far away from the school. Some of the boys simply lost interest in obtaining an education and quietly took their place among the farmers.

I had gone to school for only three or four months when a team of people came from the District Supervisor's Office to inspect the school. We were not told the details of the inspection, but in the end the headmaster called my guidance boy Harrison and let him know that I could not continue because I was underage. So that evening, Harrison went to my father and explained the problem. Both my family and I were disappointed, but no one could question the decision.

However, I was determined to continue my learning. Since I could not attend that school, I decided instead to hang around with the other boys in the evenings while they did their class assignments. There was no electricity, so most of the boys did their assignment before dark

– finishing around 6:00 or 7:00 p.m. By associating with these guys and listening to their group discussions, I learned to say and write the 26 letters of the English alphabet, count and write from one to hundred, and to do some simple addition. I never went back to that school, even when I finally was of age, because of a brand new opportunity.

In 1968, at the age of ten, I was able to attend Cocopa Plantation School. The Cocopa Plantation was operated by the Dutch that had established an elementary school to serve the employees' school-age children. My stepbrother (Big Saye) was an employee at "Division Three" at the plantation working in an unskilled labor position. He was married and suggested to my parents that I come and live with him and his wife. Since I was a relative of a plantation worker, I was eligible to go to the school as a student. I would live now only about half a mile from the Division Three School.

The school was quite different from my first Western school. The school uniforms were short green pants and white T-shirts. They also provided textbooks for the students. I received three textbooks -one each for math, reading, and science. The plantation had dug wells for the workers so I could now take my bath *before* heading off to school. The punishment for minor offenses and misbehavior was also modest which was a vast contrast to my old school was. There were many girls and boys. Everyone was excited about being in the school and dedicated to getting a serious education. I was so glad that I had come to this school.

My teacher, Olive Johnson, was probably in her late 30s. She taught kindergarten and first grade. Everyone referred to her as "teacher Johnson." She was unmarried but had several girls living in her house. Some of them were related to her and spoke the language of the Bassa tribe, an ethnic group from the coast near Monrovia. She also had girls from other tribal groups staying with her as well.

From the very beginning, I became one of her favorite students, and she quickly acknowledged me ahead of my peers. Most of the children in the class communicated well in English, as I did, but my work was always on time. I rarely misbehaved or talked in class, unlike many of the other children that the teachers found acting up. On countless occasions, when I had a shortage of pencils or notebooks, she bought those items for me. You might say, in Western terms, that I was a "teacher's pet."

At the end of the first semester, teacher Johnson recommended me for a "double promotion" which meant I went from kindergarten to grade one, and then by the end of the second semester I was promoted to the second grade. This informal education with the boys in the village and my brief time at Karnwee Elementary school prepared me very well for the Cocopa Plantation School. These experiences gave me a head start and great advantage in my new school. In 1969, I started the second grade class, but by the end of the first semester I was asked to go to the third grade class. By the end of the second semester I progressed to the fourth grade.

My situation did not stay stable for long, however, because by 1970 my stepbrother and his wife had serious marital problems. As a result, my stepbrother's wife asked me to move out of the house. I moved back to the village but continued to walk to school. The distance was now twice the distance to the Karnwee Elementary! At first, I stood up to the challenge and walked the distance, but then the months from August to September became the worst rainy period in quite some time. Most of the small rivers overflowed and my attendance became irregular. Sometimes I was only able to attend class twice or three times a week and it became very difficult to keep up with my studies.

But again, at the time unknown by me, God was proving to be faithful by bringing to me another educational opportunity. I met another boy my age, but a little taller, and we became good friends. His father had a job as an electrician, a junior staff position with the company. Their house was bigger and nicer than my stepbrother's. Robert Joseph had his own room with electricity to help him study after dark. One day he introduced me to his parents and asked if I could share his room with him. He told me, though that I would have to help with work around the house, with washing dishes, doing laundry, and drawing water from the hand-pump.

His parents agreed to let me stay with their family. Their home was comfortable and, more importantly, close to school. This situation helped me excel in school during the period from 1970 to 1973.

Although I didn't realize it at the time, the move away from my village to share a room with Robert proved for me to be an escape from death. In 1973, a measles epidemic broke out in our village and swept through the entire village. More than a dozen precious small children and several teenagers died during this epidemic. When the disease had subsided, four of my siblings were gone – dead. The epidemic broke out in the months of April and May, but the heartbreaking news was not shared with me so that I would not return to the village. In that same year my maternal grandmother Lekulah died too. These incredible losses left my mother very devastated, sick, and helpless – so much so that I was afraid that she was going to die.

In order to care for my mother, I dropped out of school and returned to the village. I came back to help her with her farm work. When the farm work slowed down, I took a job. The money I earned while working was used to purchase some necessities and gifts for her.

     *   *   *   *   *   *   *   *   *   *   *   *

During this time, I joined several boys from our village as we walked to another village about five miles away. We saw a documentary film there on the life of Samuel ("Sammy") Morris called "Angel in Ebony." Sammy, like us, was a Liberian. His desire was to share what he learned with others in Liberia. We did not understand what was meant by his desire to share the 'Holy Spirit' with others, but we learned from the film that the missionaries told Sammy that he needed as much education as he could get and that he needed to obtain this education in America. We, like Sammy, had no idea what or where America was. However, from that time on, I was driven to get as much education as I could because in my mind it was the only way to better one's self and one's family and to help others.

When my mother fully recovered in 1975, I returned to school. Because my academic performance excelled, I was promoted to grade six just two years after I returned to school. In 1976 I sat for the middle school eligibility examination and successfully passed it to start the seventh grade.

Chapter 3   From Junior High School to Marriage and High School

When I had finished the sixth grade, I had advanced beyond the highest level of education then available in the elementary schools in our region. If I wanted to further my education I would have to move to the city. The best schools with the most qualified teachers in the area were those in the LAMCO consolidated school system. Another friend and I discussed the situation and we then made plans to move to LAMCO, a city built by the American Iron Ore Corporation.

LAMCO is a contraction of the Liberian-American Iron Ore Corporation. In 1954, the government of Liberia gave 70 years of concessions to the Liberian-American-Minerals Company to explore iron ore in the area around Yekepa, a town in northern Liberia near the Guinean border. A year later, a Swedish group joined the exploration project as partners and the company was renamed Liberian-American-Swedish Minerals Company, or LAMCO. By 1963, the cities of Yekepa and Buchanan had become "company towns." The construction of the Nimba Railroad and harbor works supported the mining and transport of iron ore. The workers in those towns lived in modern homes with electricity, running water, and indoor plumbing.

Unfortunately, when we traveled there, we found that the LAMCO schools also had a policy that only employees' children could enter their school system. This was a big disappointment, but I tried to find a way to make the best of it. Since LAMCO was a company town, you could only live there if you worked there or were closely related to someone who did work there. There was a commercial city named Camp Four on the outskirts of Yekepa-LAMCO, about 5 to 7 miles out of town. Many who came to seek a job or attempt to do business with LAMCO would stop and live there while waiting for an opportunity to present itself. So, I stopped in Camp Four and quickly found a religious private school, St. Samuel's High School. Since it seemed like a potentially good alternative to the company school, I visited it and even managed to speak with the Principal about my educational aspirations.

Sei – Early in His Education

The principal took me to the proprietor of the school. The proprietor asked if I was hard working and then asked if I would work for him. He and his wife had five little children and needed help with laundry and other tasks. I told him I would be glad to work for him if he could give me a scholarship in exchange for work. He agreed to my suggestion and sent me to interview with his wife. In the end, we agreed that I would wash dishes, do the household laundry, and prepare the little children for school in the afternoon. After a while, they trusted me with purchasing food and gave me small tips every week for my hard work. The proprietor also gave another boy and me a room in their rental property apart from their residence. This gave us more freedom.

I was fortunate to be able to complete the seventh through ninth grades at St. Samuel's High School. At the end of ninth grade, I sat for the national exams and passed.

While in Camp 4 the most important event in my life happened. I met Yah Bee who later became my wife and the mother of my children! I was nineteen years old at that time in August of 1997. I will interrupt the story of my education and describe how Yah came into my life and ended up as my wife.

Here's the account of how we met. One evening, my roommate received two lady visitors. We both politely welcomed them into our place and offered them some light snacks. The older girl was the one who knew my friend, while Yah simply accompanied her friend for the visit that night. Before they left our house, I took the older girl aside and asked her about her beautiful friend. I asked questions like, "Is she married?" "Does she have a boyfriend?" "What about her character?" When the visit ended, the two young ladies left our apartment. My friend and I began reflecting on the visit trying to analyze the mystery girl. Actually, there was something unusual about her since she was so quiet and observant. She was quietly observing us to the extent that one might even have thought that she was hired by a security agency to investigate us.

After a couple of days, my friend and I decided to try again to see the two girls, but when we asked about Yah we were told that she was not at home but was selling food at the flea market. So, we quickly made our way to the flea market and there she was! She was selling food items such as roasted corn, cassava, and hot soup. We invited her, along with her friend, for a second visit. This time I really began thinking through how I would approach Yah. I created and rehearsed in my mind several things to talk about including some more personal questions that I would ask her.

The day finally arrived and we waited somewhat impatiently for their arrival that evening. Finally, we heard a knock on the door. Once again the girls entered and Yah assumed the same quiet demeanor. After some time in conversation had passed, I asked her if I could talk to her outside alone for a few minutes. Her friend quickly gave her the okay and Yah reluctantly rose out of her seat and walked outside with me. I wasted no time and started asking her every question that I had planned and rehearsed, "Are you married?" "Do you have a boyfriend?" "Where is home for you?" She told me that she was not married. She said that she had had a boyfriend but had broken up with him the year before and that she had a daughter named Olivia. She also explained to me that she was from a village about 60 miles away.

I learned that she was in town only because the rice harvest season had just ended and her mother had given her some food items to take to her brother. Her brother was working as a contractor at the LAMCO mine. After spending about a month in town she would return to her village. When she had arrived in the city, she had some money left over and decided that she would sell various items at the market until she was ready to return home. Her creativity and industriousness impressed me.

Before the evening had ended, I boldly managed to ask her if she would be my girlfriend. She replied, "but you do not know me and I do not know you yet. Besides, my brother would not approve of my having a boyfriend. He prefers that I spend my spare time with my female friends." Nonetheless, I was not deterred by her less than enthusiastic response but continued on with follow-up questions. As the evening progressed, she began to open up little-by-little. Occasionally, she would enter into a lively and great conversation sharing stories about her village, her life, her friends, her love for her mother, and her little baby that she left behind. I was making progress.

Later, one evening, Yah surprised us. We heard a knock at our door and I went to the door to see who was there. To my amazement, there she was, standing at the door alone! She handed me some food and said, "It is for you and your friend. I will not enter. I have to return to the business." The bowl contained a mixture of well-prepared food. There was fried fish in hot sauce, rice, and other tasty ingredients. The food was incredibly delicious, and was the highlight of our entire week.

After I received this gift of food, I diligently focused all my energy on pursuing Yah. I envisioned how I would one day marry her and love her forever. I was also very careful not to do anything that would upset the brother! I made sure that my friend did not change his mind and start showing an interest in her. I strongly warned him to stay away from this girl because I was going to marry her. He tried to argue with me and said, "What if her parents do not agree?" "What if she really does have a boyfriend and is just pretending to be available?" I told him that this was none of his business.

Then, I devised a plan to visit Yah's village during our upcoming break from school. I felt that her parents would be more tolerant than the city brother, who had little interest in what a great loving husband I might be to his dear sister! Before her time in town ended, I visited Yah almost every evening in the market where she worked. All too soon her visit to town ended and she returned to her village.

Before she left, though, I made arrangements to visit her village and meet her parents. My plan was coming together! In less than two weeks I began the journey to her home. Upon arrival at her village, I stopped and spoke to a middle-aged lady who owned a small grocery store there. I inquired about Yah, her character, her parents, siblings, etc. The lady spoke very highly of her. She also said, "She is quiet, polite, hard working, respectful, and close to her mother." This confirmed what I already had believed to be true about her character.

Unfortunately, the only way to the farm where Yah's family lived nine months of the year was a two-hour walk on a bush path and there were no cars or buses from the village. I got directions and set out on the journey. I walked so fast that I got to the farm within about ninety minutes and I found Yah and her mother. Yah introduced me to her mother as the boy she had spoken about. The mother thanked me for visiting and said that when her daughter had returned from the city she had spoken highly of me. Yah offered me some food.

As I was enjoying the food, her father returned from visiting a friend in a nearby village and introduced himself as Moses Bee. He had a Kpelle ethnic background. Kpelle are one of the largest ethnic groups in central Liberia. Moses was Yah's stepfather. Her biological father had passed away when she was only three years old. Moses and Yah's mother had one boy child together. Immediately, Moses began to quiz me about what I did for a living, about my home clan and about my parents. In one of my answers to a question, I happened to mention that my father was Chief Buor from Riverview town. He acknowledged that he had heard about the chief, but had never met him. He paused, looked at me and then asked the question, "What is the purpose of your visit?"

As I expressed an interest in Yah and told him about myself, he suddenly became enraged and commanded me to leave his village. I had mentioned that I was a student and immediately he reacted negatively. As far as Mr. Bee was concerned, I was not the type of prospective husband he expected his stepdaughter to bring home! His expectation was that Yah would bring home a wealthy man, not some poor boy that was still in school and, more importantly, one that had no job!

As he raised his voice louder and louder, I could hear another voice in the background telling me, "Do not leave; the village is not for him alone." Then I saw Yah's mother speaking face-to-face with her husband, challenging him to then do the same to her as what he intended to do to this strange boy. Almost immediately Moses' voice began to calm down until he became so very quiet that you would have thought he had dropped dead. Mother Gorma (Yah's mother) also lowered her voice and said, "Moses don't you remember we have three boys? Are you aware that the very way you are treating this stranger will be the way our boys will be treated the day they find someone who captures their hearts? Let me tell you one final thing that you might not know. My ancestors taught me that whatever you do in this life, you will create an equal payback for your deeds."

Then she turned to me, "My son, we are sorry; this will never happen again. Moses is a good man and he has cared for and provided food for these children since the death of my first husband. Yah also loves Moses and me very much, and we love her so much that we do not want any man to disappoint her again." Then she pointed at Yah's daughter who was almost two years old. Throughout the ordeal, Yah never spoke once.

I accepted the apology and asked if I could spend the night in the village because I wanted to give them a special "gift." I informed her that I would like to plant a small garden of cassava for them in a section of their property. Secondly, I wanted to cut down a nearby palm tree to make some wine for relaxation for them after a hard day's work. They granted my request and I arose very early in the next morning and began planting the cassava. In the afternoon I took their axe and cut down a very tall palm tree nearby. Once the tree was on the ground, I prepared it so that it would produce wine for Mother Gorma and her husband. In our culture palm wine is something that is made to be shared with others. It would provide an opportunity for Yah's family to share some with the villagers as a result of my industriousness. When these two jobs were done, I said farewell and started on the road to return home. My hope was that I made a lasting impression.

I returned to my village that evening with plans to break the news to my mother about the girl of my heart. After showing some signs that I had something special to share, my mother acknowledged me and said, "Do you have something special to talk about?"

I replied, "yes," and wasted no time. I told my whole story about visit the visit to Yah's village. Her first question was, "Why this girl?" She then said, "Is there no woman of beauty in this village or in this clan? Why must you go over to another clan to find a wife?" She seemed very disappointed in me.

She explained that the women of that clan were known for their failure to make a lifetime commitment to men. She pointed to a couple of examples of women from Yah's clan who had walked away when their husbands became sick and were no longer able to provide for their needs. However, she finished by saying, "I will honor your choice, but we first must learn about their particular family history." I promised my mother that she would be happy with this girl and explained how the shopkeeper in the neighborhood had spoken highly of Yah's character.

Since my mother was concerned about the family's history, I was determined to find some things out for myself. Before heading back to Yah's village a few weeks later, I stopped in town to investigate a little more. Unfortunately, I found that only Yah's mother had remained married; her mother's four other sisters had all divorced! I began to think more seriously about what my mother had said. Could this actually be the true history of these people? But, I quickly brushed it off and concluded that Yah was very distinct from all of the other girls of her clan after all. Secondly, Mother Gorma is the only woman married and her daughter could be just like the mother.

I headed for Yah's village that evening to check on the cassava garden and the wine tree. I spent two days this time and returned home. I concluded that I would accept the risk and marry this lady as my lifetime wife and partner. I promised myself that I would love her so much that I would give her no opportunity to even consider divorce, even if divorce was like a curse on their clan.

On arrival back in my village, I shared the news with my father. He directed me to tell his oldest son who would represent him as my father in the matter. My stepbrother, then, made a visit to Yah's village and Moses received him warmly. They all enjoyed the wine that I had processed. The wine had also become the talk of the village as mother Gorma invited several of her friends to drink it. She introduced me as Yah's friend "from a distance." She proudly pointed to the small cassava garden and the wine as marks of my productivity, hard work, and creativity. The garden and wine served as symbols of the care I would take of Yah.

Before my father's representative left the village, he made it clear that he wanted a private closed-door meeting with Moses and his wife. He clarified his mission and long-term intentions, which primarily pointed to their daughter's relationship with me. He concluded the meetings by letting them know that he desired to invite not only Yah but also the whole village to see our village and our family. He further explained that he did not know when he would arrange the visit but that, if their daughter suddenly disappeared, they should not be alarmed but they could consider him to be a prime suspect! My plan was beginning to come together!

About this time school resumed. After about a month, I received a message from my mother that Yah had come to see them and wanted me to come home to our village while she was still there. I took a weekend off and went home. When I arrived that evening, my mother called me behind closed doors and explained that she did not think it was appropriate for me to marry a woman from another region and that she remained concerned about the history of that region. I managed to convince her that Yah's and her mother's history was particularly unique and that I wanted to pursue the path of marriage. I also explained how Yah's mother had become my "heroine" during the encounter with her husband. In return, my mother responded that she would support our marriage and gave me her special blessings for our future including our future children. My father also blessed me that night and offered a traditional prayer for a bright future.

When Yah returned to her village both her mother and father had a closed-door talk with her. They blessed her and gave her their support to marry me if she thought I was the right husband for her. Her parents assured her that they were in no hurry for her to leave their home and told her they would support her and meet all her needs as long as they both lived.

After that we decided to move forward with the preparations for our marriage. We arranged a basic traditional marriage since at the time the two of us were non-believers. When the appointed time arrived, my parents joined me and we went to Yah's people. All the distant relatives were invited and everyone assembled in the town on the day of our arrival. In the evening, our chief spokesperson got up and introduced our group and Yah's family's spokesperson did the same thing. The process was tedious since traditional African marriages have strict patterns which must be followed. Within about two or three hours we exchanged gifts with Yah's parents. This was followed by a celebration over wine and food.

Yah and I returned to my village that night for our honeymoon. Since school was still in session, I came back to the village every other weekend to see her. During that time Yah and my mother became close friends. She loved my mother and helped with the farm work. She proved herself to be a hard-working, productive, and business-minded person. She started a small business from her room selling peanuts, kerosene, and pepper. Soon she became known in the whole village and the surrounding areas. Everyone spoke about her respect for both old and young people, of her quietness, and of her productivity.

*   *   *   *   *   *   *   *   *   *   *   *

From the beginning I vowed never to physically abuse her. The Lord greatly helped me to uphold these promises when we both became believers in Jesus. We now have the Bible to turn to when we have conflicts. Whenever there was a conflict, we would put the children to bed and move into our room to read the Bible. We very often read from the letter of the Apostle Paul to the Ephesians. We particularly read chapters five and six concerning Paul's admonition that a husband should love his wife as Jesus did the Church and that a wife should submit to her husband.

We have been married for over thirty years and we have kept these promises to ourselves and prayed to strengthen our relationships in Christ, to one another, and to our children. We are not perfect. We still have disagreements like any other married couple but never allow such arguments to continue without trying to resolve them. I affectionately call Yah, "Madam," from "mademoiselle" (for a young French woman). A short period of time after we converted, Yah and I were formally confirmed as a Christian married couple.

As part of his goodness to us, the Lord has blessed our family with five lovely children and a grandson. Our children are Olivia, Lily, Tonzia, Deizie, and Benjamin. They are both our treasure (and our challenge) as we bring them up in the discipline of the Lord. Our grandson is named Saye (the original spelling of my name).

*   *   *   *   *   *   *   *   *   *   *   *

Now, back to the story of my education. It should now be clear, the pursuit of education was a driving force in my life. I had worked very hard and sacrificed a great deal to get the education I had already achieved and I was willing to sacrifice more in the future, if necessary.

In 1978, when I first heard about Sanniquellie Central High School (S.C.H.S.) and that it was the most prestigious and best public high school built by the government, I knew right away that I wanted to attend that school. The school was located in Sanniquellie, the school headquarters for all of Nimba County. The dream of thousands of young men and women from Nimba County was to attend S.C.H.S. The main purpose of this high school was to educate the future leaders of our county and our country. The students there interacted regularly with political leaders. The most successful business people and politicians came from this school.

In order for me to attend S.C.H.S., I had to overcome two obstacles. First, I had to pass the entrance examination. The second challenge was providing our own food. These basic entrance requirements are probably not perceived as a challenge by most Western high school students, but they could prove a real challenge for me. The entrance exam covered math, science, and English, and only the best students were eligible. I joined a group of students who were committed to being accepted and we approached the task seriously. First of all, one of our group members specifically visited the school to secretly interview some of the current students about the test. Then, based on that report, we created an outline of what would be covered and divided the material among the members of the group. Each member performed intensive research and outlined his material in preparation for us to study individually and together. After about three months of study, we felt that we were all prepared to take the examination.

The day before the examination, the three of us got on the bus and went to Sanniquellie. We spent the night in the city. This was my first night in this city. I had passed through once before on my way to LAMCO but had never stopped. I did, however, see the school edifice from a distance. There was nothing fancy about the building itself. It was built in an "L" shape and painted a light yellow color. The yard was kept very clean and was attractively landscaped. One unusual feature was the flagpole in front of the building. It was twice the height of any of the flagpoles that I had seen at my former schools.

The next morning everyone woke up and got ready for the test. We found a little water to wash our faces, but took no showers and had no breakfast. No one was hungry or even cared about breakfast. We were too anxious about taking the test. The test began at 9:00 a.m. but we got there about an hour early to glean every last bit of information and strategy we could before taking the test. The atmosphere on the campus was extremely calm as every student was on his best behavior. Literally, there were thousands of students. There was someone from almost every village and from all over Nimba County. I knew a couple of them from my old schools, but there was not much time for friendly conversation. We all had to be ready to start the test.

Finally, the principal, Sei Kokeh, appeared and gave instructions for everyone to assemble by the flagpole. He had us line up like a military unit ready for inspection. There was something that I quickly noticed about this Mr. Kokeh. His name indicated that he was from the Mano tribal group to which I belonged, except he spelled his name differently. The common spelling was "Saye" but he spelled his name "Sei." Later on I changed my name from the traditional spelling of Saye, to Sei. Most of the other "Sayes" did so as well. There were other distinctive features and characteristics that this principal had. His voice was loud and very powerful as he gave out instructions for the test, and he expressed his expectations about our behavior in no uncertain terms. He was a large man, weighing about 300 to 350 pounds and was well-dressed including a necktie. All the other teachers were very well-dressed in neckties or in their African clothing embroidered with colorful threads; however, we discovered that only on test day and registration day was anyone allowed to come onto the campus with bright colorful clothes. I dressed in long pants and a short-sleeved shirt. Once accepted in the school, all the students understood that you would be clean and dressed in the school uniform (long khaki pants with a long-sleeved blue shirt and black tie) whenever you were on campus.

At 9:00 a.m. we were given orders to promptly go to the testing classrooms. The tests lasted for about three to four hours. We worked straight through without breaks so as to keep students from talking to each other. The test was so strictly administered that you were too intimidated to ask questions or even look up. Looking to the side at another student's test or turning around could result in your immediate disqualification from the test. There were about 60 or 75 prospective students in each of a number of classrooms set up for this test. The mood was very tense, but calm.

When the bell rang to signal the end of the testing period, every student immediately stood up and, in single file, walked out of the classrooms. We had previously been instructed that the names of those who passed the test would be posted on the campus bulletin board in about three to four weeks. There was no guaranteed date, but they did add that there would be an announcement on the radio when the results were posted. Everyone returned to their homes and waited eagerly for the announcement. Some of those that could afford the transportation cost would come into town to check for their names several times during this waiting period, but I could not afford to do so, so I did not even try.

Finally, the announcement came on the radio. My two friends came by to pick me up to go check our results, but I declined thinking that I likely had not passed the test. I had no desire to spend the 75 cents for transportation just to get the bad news! So they left without me and returned that evening. One of the two friends came back extremely excited and told me he had passed, but what really surprised me was when he said that I had passed also! Our other friend, unfortunately, did not pass. He fell short by just a few points.

The next day I did spend the 75 cents to go to the city just to satisfy myself that I had really passed. When I arrived on the campus, I went right to the bulletin board. The names were listed in alphabetical order and sure enough there was my name "Sei Buor" right near the top of the list. I was now a candidate for the most prestigious school in Nimba County.

So in 1978 I entered the Sanniquellie Central High School, my dream school. I was determined to do everything required in order to be successful. To me, that meant I would keep my grade point average as high as possible. I knew this would require adequate preparation and hard work.

My next task was preparing to move to the city. It was an exciting time for me. Housing was not a difficult problem because the government had given half of a building lot to every clan for the purpose of constructing housing for their future students. So, our clan had a house already built. Our clan house had three bedrooms and a big family room for studying. The only problem was that many students would have to live in a single room. This meant that I ended up sharing a room with five other boys from our clan. The girls did the same thing.

Most of the girls were maturing and very beautiful. They soon found boyfriends to support and entertain them. On weekends they would spend time with their boyfriends by going into Lamco where their boyfriends would join them. From the gifts and support they received the girls generously shared their blessings with us.

In return for this help, we washed their clothes and helped them with assignments – since they were too busy to do all of their work. Two particular girls, Alice and Martha, became known for their extreme generosity. These two girls became housemothers for the other students. In return we did everything we could to help, honor, and protect them. In my second year, Martha's grade point fell below the acceptable standard and she was dropped from Central High but she later entered a private school and eventually completed high school. Today, Martha lives in

Minnesota and is happily married. Alice is also married and works at the Roberts International Airport in Monrovia, Liberia.

After a successful school year in grade 10, I was ready for the junior year. By then I had also built friendships with both new and old students and with many professors. I ran for a position on the student council and was elected. I represented students at important faculty meetings and at conferences with county political leaders. In my senior and final year in high school I became a social minister in the student council. I coordinated all the bands and social events for the school. Unfortunately this socializing led me into drinking alcoholic beverages and smoking the prestigious "Benson and Hedges" cigarettes. Nonetheless, I continued to excel in my studies and graduated on December 18, 1980. I was able to fulfill my goal of keeping my grades high throughout the years except during times of illness.

This had been a long journey for me. I had attended four schools. I had lived with friends, relatives, and on my own. I had done laundry and odd jobs and sometimes walked 20 miles a day to class. I had done all of this to pursue my education. I was proud of what I had accomplished and my family was also proud of me. I thought of the future and what I would do with all that I had learned. In my mind I had not just done this for myself. I wanted to have a chance to help others and I believed that this would happen. I wanted to show that education in general and my education in particular would have a useful impact on our society.

Chapter 4   God Calls Us

A year before my graduation from high school, I had begun to wonder about the purpose of my life. I pondered such questions as, "What should I do with my life after graduation?" and "What are my ultimate goals in life?" The main purpose of Sanniquellie Central High School was to prepare young people to become successful government and business leaders so I was trying to figure out what precise type of career path to take. I was interested, however, in helping my people and positively impacting the world in some special way. I just could not figure out exactly what would be the best way for me to accomplish these personal goals. Further education would be in my plan, but I did not know where or with what emphasis.

My parents practiced traditional African religious beliefs. These beliefs and practices emphasized the supernatural and community harmony. We believed that everything in life is directly influenced by the world of the spirits. We also believed that our own actions in the physical world had a direct impact on the spiritual world. The correct response to any physical life situation is a spiritual one whether it's a matter of family affairs, sickness, or ceremonial practices.

Therefore, given this worldview, the essential quest is to understand the secret of using the appropriate supernatural spiritual power to help us in any problem of life. Failure to properly use such power led to great anxiety. In other words, life without power is not really worth living. To obtain the appropriate power one has to perform rituals including sacrifices, offerings, taboos, fetishes, and other ceremonies.

For the most part, the spirits are those of one's ancestors. That is why it is so important to know one's clan history and to appeal to the ancestors that were most powerful when you needed good things to happen. The rituals I remember the most is the "planting ritual." My father would gather all his wives and children, kill a chicken, and call on the good spirits to bless our farming season. Each season he would call on the same spirits when the harvest was plentiful and remind them of all they had done for us and how good they had been to us. After pouring the chicken's blood out on the ground as part of the ritual, we would all go home and have a chicken dinner. Since I was not living in our farming community, I had not taken part in that ceremony for several years.

Community harmony is a very important part of our tribal life. This concept embodies the principle that man is not merely an individual but that his real life is in community with others. In fact, each individual is considered to be incomplete and inadequate without the whole community. The individual only feels important when he has the support of the community. If a relationship is broken between members of the same group, this serious breach in relationships is considered a "sin."

To be recognized as a full functioning member of our society, one needed to be in good relationships with not only the living members of the community, but also those ancestors who had died. Your ancestors, especially the more recent dead, are considered to be an essential part of the community. A man's power was measured by the influence these ancestors had over his daily life. Without them, a man would lose his focus and reason (or meaning) for living and so would be rendered powerless. Community was designed to be lived in harmony; therefore, whatever actions and beliefs encourage the maintenance of this harmony, such as private and community rituals, supported and strengthened the community.

We all feared withdrawing from the society or creating undue negative publicity. Diversity or non-conformity is costly to the community and may signal the activity of demon spirits, which spirits could bring curses on the entire community or household.

The practice of African traditional religion is very self-centered. One prays, implores the ancestors, and makes sacrifices, not out of devotion, but in order to manipulate the spirit world. He venerates the divine and his ancestors for his own purposes, and he promotes harmony and order in his environment so that he can accomplish his personal goals, which includes the maintenance of good health for family members (prevention of sickness and natural disasters) and general protection from evil spirits. To worship other gods would invite the anger of the ancestors which could lead to these ancestors sending curses on the offender or even all of his family members.

*   *   *   *   *   *   *   *   *   *   *   *

One afternoon after leaving school, I began walking home. On the way I met a local Christian evangelist named Amos Miamen who was sitting along a small foot path. Amos was a student at the African Bible College. He deliberately sat along a dusty bush path where students passed by so he could share the good news of God's love for them. The footpath was near the City Gate house where students often gathered.

Many years later, I asked Amos about our meeting. Amos told me that he was there because he had once been in a taxicab with several Sanniquellie Central High School students. They had been discussing Liberian politics and he brought up the topic, "God and the person of Jesus."

Amos said that one of them had been quiet while he explained our spirit world heritage. Amos arranged to meet him the next Saturday to continue the discussion. "Sei, you showed up and became more interested in the discussion than the person who invited me," Amos told me.

Amos continued, "The early eighties were the years of radical politics in Liberia. It was a time of independent thinking and political revolution. You approached the discussion from a purely intellectual and nationalistic angle. But I saw in you an ally who was helping me to explain my faith to a listening audience that normally would not listen to me."

Amos's message was based on a famous Bible verse. "For God so loved the world that he gave his one and only Son, that whoever believes in him shall not perish but have eternal life" (John 3:16). The text emphasized the sacrificial death of Jesus and His Father's love for the world, and that included me, Sei Buor. At that time, I couldn't imagine someone giving up his only son for someone else or someone giving his own life for someone else.

When Amos ended his message, I started to walk away, but he stopped me and asked if he could visit me the next time he came to town. I reluctantly pointed in the general direction of my village in such a manner that let Amos know that it was very far away. I didn't really think he was serious about visiting me. Furthermore, I thought he could never find me anyway. So I thought I was safe from that evangelist! However, to my total dismay, Amos appeared the following week. He began looking for me in the spot where we first met and knocked on several doors asking others where I lived in the community. In the end, Amos found me.

For several weeks he came by to see me whenever he was in town. In my ignorance, I was rebellious toward the God who had created me in His own image. It took me several weeks to understand who God was and what he had done for me.

I wanted to do my own thing and control my own life and I tried to hide in the darkness of my sins, not wanting to deal with this eternal holy God. I realized that I now was exercising my will in choosing to resists God. In essence, I decided I would turn down God's invitation to be His child and would reject fellowship with Him. Like Adam and Eve, the first pair of human beings that God created, I also tried to hide from God.

However, God decided not to take "no" for an answer. He knows the dangers, pitfalls, and disasters that lurk in the darkness of this world. In His love for me He began to draw me towards Himself. God used Amos as His messenger to pursue me.

One day I walked Amos to the bus stop so that he could catch the bus back to his college, which was some forty miles away. As we waited for the next bus to arrive, Amos turned to me and asked, "Sei, is there any reason that would prevent you from accepting Jesus into your life?" I responded, "No!" He then asked me if I would like to accept Jesus into my life on that day and I immediately responded, "Yes." He suggested that we go back to my campus, which was not very far from the city center, and pray together.

When we arrived on the campus, we found an open classroom, knelt down and prayed. Amos actually led me through the prayer and I repeated it after him. I specifically prayed asking God to forgive me of my sins and for Jesus to become my Savior and Lord.

Amos explained to me that God had provided the only way to remove our sin through the death of Jesus Christ on the cross. Amos shared about God's grace, a new concept for me. He shared further that the Bible tells us, "…because of his great love for us, God, who is rich in mercy, made us alive with Christ even when we were dead in transgressions; it is by grace you have been saved." (Ephesians 2:4-5). From that moment on, I believed that God had pardoned my sins and forgiven me.

Amos was thrilled that I had become a Christian. He has since told me, "You cannot imagine how I felt to have led a person to Christ." The evangelism work Amos did was part of his practical curriculum at African Bible College.

Although my life was plagued by confusion, God in His love had mercy on me. He forgave me and delivered me from my sins. The Scriptures tell us that, "He who has the Son has life, but he who does not have the Son does not have life." (1 John 5:12-13). This verse gave me the assurance that I needed as the basis for the new life in Christ I received that day.

For several years following my conversion, Amos and his wife Mary, discipled and trained me in a local church. They took me under their wings and gave me the protection, mentoring, and even parenting which I lacked since I had left my parents to go far away to Sanniquellie High School to complete my studies.

I also joined a youth group in the city and studied the Scriptures on a weekly basis. Through these weekly studies and meetings, it became clear to me that Jesus is the Truth and the Way to His father and eternal life. I could believe in Him and His promises and put my life in His trust. (John 14:6; Hebrews 10:19-20; Acts 18:26). I soon joined a local church and began worshipping with other believers.

With Christ as my Lord and Savior, I was no longer fearful that curses or evil spirits would harm me. These fears seemed to melt away because Jesus Christ gave me a new hope that included eternal life after death. Many of my non-believing friends had nothing to do with me after my conversion and some openly rejected or ridiculed me. I continued, however, to press onward and I never looked back.

When I accepted Jesus as my Savior, my father felt I betrayed him and he was terribly disappointed in me. He became angry and quit talking to me for quite a long time. I made several attempts to explain my changed life and tried to share Christ with him, but he would frequently remind me that my God was a "white man's god." My family felt especially betrayed since I was my mother's first born. My father had always counted on me to look after the family's land when he got older and now I had betrayed him in this responsibility. He sincerely believed that my betrayal would not only harm me but it would be detrimental to other members of his families. (Remember, he had six wives each with several children.)

One of my early prayers was for God to transform my life in such a way that I would be able to faithfully and effectively serve him and for Him to use me to His glory. I began to invite mature Christians into our village to help me become bold in my witness for Jesus Christ. Eventually my mother and other friends came to accept the Lord.

God sought and found me and brought me into fellowship with Him. I was not looking for God nor expecting Him, but He came at the right time when I needed Him most and was sensitive to hearing the Good News. God wanted me to know Him personally and speak to Him directly. I knew that I no longer needed to go through my ancestors for help. Before I was a Christian I perpetually lived in fear of mistreating our ancestors and coming under their curses in which they could allow evil spirits to hurt our family. I was so thankful to God that He had delivered me from this superstitious past.

In the early years following my salvation, the Lord promised to restore what I had lost during my time of testing when it seemed like I was rejected by all my family and friends (Joel 2:25-28). God has faithfully shown me that when I trust him in the difficult trials He will eventually use me to powerfully impact those in my sphere of influence. He has answered my prayers and blessed me with good health, a great family, wonderful guidance, and many opportunities for ministry.

I now had a mission to help my people in Liberia. I continued to prepare myself for what was ahead. I knew that the simple message of the Lordship of Christ and his gracious saving work on the cross and a total trust in God's written Word, would enable me to fulfill my God-given mission.

In 1981, I sensed a calling to join the staff of the United Liberia Inland Church Academy (a high school) to teach Liberian civics, history, and English in a Christian atmosphere. It was during this period that I was mentored by another man of God, Rev. David Carson (a missionary with Worldwide Evangelization for Christ International, WEC). "Pop Carson," as he was affectionately called by students, was able to answer my theological and biblical questions, and he prayed with me whenever I was in need. Since I was his translator in the villages during preaching trips, I informally learned how to share the gospel with my own people. Rev. Carson, an Irishman, had been among the first group of eight missionaries that came to Liberia in 1938. He and his wife Maud had helped establish the Liberia Inland Mission, a middle school, and a medical clinic. He continued to mentor Liberian Christians until 1988.

Since then, and for the past twenty years of my life, I have found the art of preaching and teaching God's word to my own clan to be a fascinating and challenging task. My present interest in preaching and teaching was definitely strengthened through my interaction with Amos and Mary Miamen. The call of God on my life was so clear and compelling that I had no difficulty sticking with this calling, even during the period when my peers ridiculed me. They later began to commend me when they saw that I was unwavering in my decision to follow Christ.

Yah's family had attended a Methodist Church when she was growing up, so she was familiar with the Bible. Her family was not very involved with the spirit worship and rituals because they considered themselves to be Christians. During the time I was teaching at the United Liberia Inland Church Academy, Yah was asked to join a Bible study.

Yah says: "I went and listened attentively every week. I asked questions. Sometimes I answered questions. For the first time, I really understood the Bible." The Bible was a Mano translation which contextualized the Bible stories for our culture, making them more meaningful to the Mano people.

One day they read Luke 17:34, "I tell you, on that night two people (the Mano version says 'a man and his wife') will be sleeping in one bed; one will be taken and the other left." Yah asked the leader exactly what that meant.

The leader explained that if the husband or the wife was a believer in Christ and the other was not when Christ returns, the believer would be taken and the unbeliever would be left. Yah said emphatically, "I want to be a believer now." The leader prayed with her.

As Yah explains, "I have been a different person ever since that prayer. I love to study the Bible. And I know that Sei is serving God wherever God sends him. When we are separated, I am not afraid because God is with me, and He gives me His assurance that He will take care of me and the children. God is my strength. and I will live forever with Jesus."

*   *   *   *   *   *   *   *   *   *   *   *

I have lived in the West long enough to see the how the Christian worldview influences culture. I have lived in the United States long enough to know that materialism, hedonism, and secular humanism clash with, and sometimes dilute, the Christian values upon which the United States was founded. In my homeland the clash of cultures is not between humanism and Christianity, but between animism and Christianity.

During the pre-Christian era my forefathers practiced animism. They worshiped lifeless idols as rivers, mountains, trees, and ancestors. These gods and goddesses had no breath, movement, or sight, and possess no power (Psa. 115:47; 135:15-18). I naturally grew up trusting in these gods and goddesses since I was born into that culture having no knowledge of Christ.

The God of heaven revealed himself to me in this kind of culture and family situation. In contrast to the gods of my ancestors, the true God, whom I now worship, gives eternal life and does not mislead us. God relentlessly is committed to breaking through our ignorance, redeeming us for himself, and ending our worship of vain powerless gods and goddesses carved by hands (Col. 1:15-16).

*   *   *   *   *   *   *   *   *   *   *   *

While teaching at United Liberian Inland Church Academy, I became involved with several missionaries. They asked me to teach Sunday school. I had to confess that I didn't know the Bible that well, but they patiently helped me prepare lessons. One missionary became sick and said that he and his wife would have to return home. They had been at the Academy for many years. "Who would replace them?" I thought. I definitely appreciated what they were doing for my people because they were there to help us learn about and know God. I wondered if I could do this job and really pastor these people. I would have the obvious advantage of not needing a translator, but I just didn't think I had enough knowledge of the Bible.

Early Years of Buor Family

I knew of the African Bible College, the one that Amos attended when he witnessed to me. I asked about the possibility of my attending there. I took the test and passed the New Testament portion as well as the section on competency in composition. I did not pass the Old Testament part of the test, however. Nonetheless, the missionary gave me a good reference and I was accepted.

So in 1982, after teaching for two years, in order to be able to serve the Lord in full-time ministry, I took a study leave to pursue pastoral training. Our family moved to Lamco-Yekepa, a mining city about 80 miles from the school where I had been teaching. The African Bible College was established by Presbyterian missionaries from the state of Mississippi in the U.S., but it was interdenominational. Part of our training was to do student internships like Amos had done, so I still had a chance to minister to others and practice what I was learning. I really enjoyed my studies and worked hard to graduate in four years.

In addition to not only now having a Bachelor of Arts degree, I knew that I had been better prepared to lead, whether it was in a church, in a government position, in a Christian organization, or in an institution of higher learning. I knew that I could better accomplish my dreams of ministering more effectively to my people.

Sei at African Bible College

African Bible College (ABC) focused on excellence and was considered one of the best schools in all of Liberia. It infused students with a sense of pride. Students at ABC felt the urgent need to change their traditional ways once they arrived on the campus, even before their orientation. It was a life–changing culture and powerful example of a God-centered education that transformed these students.

The academic program was developed and designed in such a way that it transformed the student's speaking skills from slang and sloppy "lingo" to sharp and fluent communication. The dress code was stricter than at previous institutions I had attended. Students wore a traditional African embroidered shirt and clean slacks or a Western-style tie with a button-down shirt tucked neatly into the slacks.

The academic standard was one of excellence. Students were taught library research and writing skills as well as rigorous interpersonal skills development from the first day to the day of graduation. Students were told they were the "cream of the crop" and were discouraged from doing or turning in any poor or lazy work. Students were expected to develop rapidly and hand in well-prepared assignments. Upon graduation, every student had complete confidence that ABC had recreated them and had made them better persons that fit into God's world. The students developed confidence to lead not only in church leadership, but also in the areas of secular leadership in business and government. Several of the graduates even went back to study law, business, and other professions. Others were open to serving with organizations outside of their own denominations or in the government.

The buildings themselves at African Bible College surpassed many religious institutions in Liberia. The construction materials and furnishings were imported from the United States. Students' facilities, dormitories, restrooms, classrooms and the entire campus were spotlessly clean all of the time.

Students receiving scholarship assistance were assigned two hours of work, five or six days per week. These students took care of the buildings grounds, trimming and mowing the grass or maintaining the classrooms, library and chapel. They also worked in the dining hall. Students with basic building skills were placed in construction work and led by a construction supervisor. There was a well-organized work force of students maintaining the campus in its pristine state!

The ABC infrastructure was designed to be "first class" so that anyone could clearly see that the school was not a place designed for poor Africans that a missionary hastily built and then abandoned. ABC was clearly a place where the missionaries invested their lives and stayed over a long period in order to establish a lasting legacy for the future of their students. Even the missionary houses reflected a nice style suitable for the faculty of an elite American school.

Graduation from ABC was more like a "commissioning" to be sent out. From African Bible College there was no expectation that the graduate would come back to teach or train other Africans. Students were not taught to mentor others. We all received the impression that ABC was all the training you would ever need. This thinking, however, was soon about to change under new leadership.

While I was attending ABC once again Yah ventured into a small business. With very little initial funding, she began selling peppers, eggplant, potatoes and grains. She sold these items in both retail and wholesale markets, and in a short time she had established herself as a permanent fixture in the local community market. Through this business, she was also able to provide income and food for our family which allowed me to focus on my studies at the college. In 1986, when I graduated from Africa Bible College, I started teaching again, and also pastoring at a church in town.

*   *   *   *   *   *   *   *   *   *   *   *

In 1994, I was fortunate enough to have a chance to go back and visit ABC. I received a warm welcome from Dr. Dell Chinchen, the new president. Dr. Dell was quick to offer congratulatory comments regarding my academic achievement at NEGST (Nairobi Evangelical Graduate School of Theology) in the interim years. He even welcomed me to take my place among his teaching staff if I ever returned to Liberia. Based on what I heard him say, it appeared that a new day had dawned at ABC in which the idea of Africans training Africans is seen as positive and necessary.

The Liberian government, through the Ministry of Higher Education, had introduced a new policy. In order to obtain government approval, an institution is required to hire national staff and also include a "national" on the institution's board. This is a positive sign for ABC to connect the missing link to its vision and the great work started in Liberia. For this, I commend the current President, Dr. Dell Chinchen. He has already embraced this strategic approach to involve Liberians in what God is doing through ABC. The Liberian civil war drove all of the missionaries back to their own countries, but some Liberian nationals remained and risked their lives to safeguard the college. Unfortunately, in 1995, the school staff was unable to withstand the attacks of the rebels who eventually burned the college down and destroyed the entire infrastructure.

Part II   Furthering My Education

Chapter 5   God Feeds and Educates

It is often said, "When God calls, he equips." But, it's sometimes possible to overlook the importance of seeking appropriate training that would enhance the particular work The Lord has called us to in our ministry.

In 1986, in my role as a pastor, I was privileged to travel to Amsterdam to attend the International Conference for Itinerant Evangelists put on by the Billy Graham Evangelistic Association (www.BillyGraham.org). Over ten thousand evangelists from almost every country in the world participated in the conference. In our lunch break after the first session, we were told to make some new friends during the prayer time.

I made my way through the crowd and sat down with a group of five people. I noticed at the table a short distinguished middle-aged man with a well-trimmed beard. He had traditional tribal marks on his cheeks and I assumed that he was from Nigeria or Ghana. Everyone became silent as we quickly ate our food to get ready for the next session of the conference. Some wanted to quickly finish eating and spend some time reading or browsing through the evangelism literature. Others wanted to take a quick nap so as to remain alert for the next session.

I heard an exciting and commanding man's voice speak out, "Gentleman, may I ask that we each introduce ourselves?" I quickly relaxed and gave this man my undivided attention. Again he said, "May we all introduce ourselves – our name, country, and service?"

I was a little shy, but one brave fellow called out his name, nationality, and vocation. He was followed by a couple more in our group. Soon, I had performed my task and we all looked at the original speaker. He said, "My name is Tokunbo Adeyemo. I am from Nigeria and I live in Nairobi, Kenya. I serve as the President (Vice Chancellor) of Nairobi Evangelical Graduate School of Theology (often referred to as NEGST and pronounced "next")." We had a brief discussion, but it quickly came to an end and we all then returned to finish our food. As we were finishing, I approached Tokunbo and asked him if I could speak privately with him. He accepted my request.

Then, in our closed-door discussion, I expressed my desire to go further with my education but that I lacked the financial means. I had only about a month before I would graduate from African Bible College and I told him that I had survived financially because I was in a work-study program. I told him that I did not have "the first penny" to pay for a plane ticket to Kenya and obviously had no money to pay for the cost of a seminary education.

Adeyemo asked for my contact information and promised to get back to me. Before we departed, he took my hand and said, "I will pray for you." He gave me these direct but encouraging words, "If God wants you to go to seminary, He will provide the funding."

About three or four weeks after the conference, I received a letter from NEGST. In the letter, the school secretary explained, "Your friend Dr. Adeyemo has asked me to send you this letter with the application form." She then urged me to fill in the form and return it in a timely manner.

I filled out the application form and indeed I did meet the admission requirements, but one serious obstacle remained. There was no funding for me in sight! Again and again I reflected on the assurance from Dr. Adeyemo about God's provision, but it was a mystery to me on how God was going to fund my education in Nairobi. I prayed about the situation and one day I shared with a good friend, Augustine Davies, the good news of both this educational opportunity and the financial obstacle I was facing. Augustine was from the nation of Sierra Leone and he and his wife, Jeneba, were students at African Bible College. Augustine and I shared an office in our work-study program as we worked in the Bible correspondence courses department. Our responsibilities were to grade students on their course work, issue certificates of completion, and send new materials to both new applicants and existing students.

Through our conversation, Augustine let me know that Tearfund, a foundation in the United Kingdom, was the source of my present funding. Since Tearfund (www.tearfund.org) worked in partnership with a variety of Christian agencies and churches worldwide, he said it was likely that I would qualify for additional funding for further education. He urged me to write them and express my gratitude for prior funding, but also to share with them that I had been accepted to NEGST (www.negst.edu) and would like to request additional help.

That night I prayed and drafted a letter to Tearfund. I allowed Augustine to proofread it and then I sent the letter to the UK. After four weeks of anxious waiting, dreaming and anticipating an answer, the letter finally arrived. Tearfund sent me a package that included a well-worded cover letter of about two or three paragraphs and a scholarship application form that I was to complete. The application also needed the signature of a local church official. Augustine and I had already formed a bond as we were persuaded that this was my best opportunity. He seriously exhorted me to write thoughtful and precise answers to every question. Tearfund receives literally thousands of inquiries every year. I knew that my application had to stand out since there would be no second chance.

After I completed my portion of the application, I came to the section that was to be completed by the local "sending" church. The church is required to help sponsor the student since the foundation does not offer a 100% scholarship. I took the materials and went to see the general secretary of the Church with this concern and his response was, "Our church is poor and we don't have the money." Unfortunately, this was not the kind of news I was looking for. This news was very disheartening.

Then I had another idea. I felt compelled to meet with the President of our denomination. I knew the chances for such a meeting were quite slim since I did not know him on a personal level. Besides, I had no relatives or close friends who were serving (or had served) in the denomination in leadership capacities that could introduce me to him. I persisted, however, to present my case to the Rev. Donald Wuanti. When I arrived at his home, I was told he had left for a speaking tour in another city.

I left quickly to find him and arrived just at the time he was about to take a break from his meeting. He pulled me aside to hear my case. I shortened my explanation and gave him my letter from Tearfund. He carefully read through it, and I could see that his elderly hands refused to hold the document in a still position. I saw his lips moving steadily from line to line. Then, I saw something else - a smile lighting his entire face as he turned to me and said, "Sei, praise God for you that He will grant us this opportunity to stand with you." Then, he said, "As Rev. McCoy (the General Secretary) has told you, we do not have money; our church is poor. But we have the Holy Spirit and prayer."

He then began to look for his pen, but I promptly produced one. He wrote a short note on a piece of paper and sent me back to the General Secretary. I did not read the letter, but the message was loud and clear. He had urged his friend Laurie McCoy to proceed with the recommendation and to sign it on behalf of the Church. He told me to let God be God as we prayed and trusted in the power of the Holy Spirit.

Since that day I have found out that prayer does indeed work! Rev. Donald Wuanti, like the Apostle James, understood that the prayer of righteous men prevails and is powerful and effective! Those words from Dr. Adeyemo and Rev. Wuanti, along with the generous support from the Tearfund, opened the way for me to attend NEGST.

Our local church (United Liberia Inland Church) granted us a study leave. After eight years of pastoring and teaching in two local churches, on September 9, 1988, my wife and I and our three children (Lily, Tonzia and Deizie) left Liberia. We went to Nairobi, Kenya, so that I could pursue a Masters in Divinity from NEGST.

In God's perfect timing we left a Liberia that would soon experience the beginning of a major civil war that would engulf the whole country. Before our departure for Nairobi, we saw "red flags" as ethnic tensions escalated in every part of the country, an indication that something was going wrong with our nation. We first saw problems when we attempted to obtain an exit visa. When I left Liberia in 1986 to attend the Itinerant Evangelists conference in Amsterdam, I was not required to have an exit visa in Liberia. This time it was different.

We received all the admission documents from NEGST and began our journey. We took public transportation to Monrovia and from there we planned to fly to Nairobi. Since we had lived in a mission station 160 miles from the capital, as we were leaving the country we realized that we were ignorant of many of the conflicts taking place between various tribal groups within Liberia. For example, we did not know that the government had taken control of all utilities since we had our own well for water. We also generated our own electricity and we grew our own food. The political situation in Liberia was quickly escalating beyond our awareness and comprehension.

Upon arrival in Monrovia, we were told we would need to obtain an exit visa before leaving the country. In the morning we drove to the government security branch in charge of issuing the visas. When we entered the immigration office, I naively submitted our passports and someone reviewed them while we waited outside. The person who took our passports came back and asked if I was leaving the country with my entire family. He wanted to know if there was any reason I needed to take my entire family with me. I replied, "No, except that the scholarship covered both my family and me." Then he went back to the boss' office. Since I was taking my whole family they somehow assumed that I was fleeing the country for some wrong I had committed. They proceeded to check and see if my name was on a variety of lists.

Not only were we naive about the various new government requirements, but we falsely believed the propaganda that this government desired to make our lives better. In fact, the new government was called "The People's Redemption Council" since we were told they "had come to redeem the indigenous people who had been repressed since the beginning of the nation of Liberia." We believed they were working for us. In reality, they were attempting to suppress everyone who was not openly committed to their regime.

We waited from 8:30 a.m. until almost noon. The employees began to walk past us on the way out to lunch and still we were not called in. By this time, we were getting a bit concerned and were wondering what was going on. But many times in Africa you have to wait, and so we waited.

Fortunately, a pregnant lady came out on her way to lunch, and Yah pointed at her and said that she looked like someone familiar from the city of Lamco where we went to College. I quickly approached and asked her if she had lived in that area before, but she said no. Not deterred, I then asked if she could help us obtain the exit visas. She agreed to petition her boss on our behalf if I would buy her lunch since she only had a limited time for her lunch break. I agreed and even

welcomed her to join our family for lunch. She went back to the boss'
office with our passports. The "lunch for passports" mechanism had
seemed like a good way of "expediting" the visa process, and we were
thankful that God led Yah to notice this woman.

While we were waiting for our passports to be processed, she began
to ask me about my profession, and I replied that I was a teacher and a
pastor. When she heard this, she thanked God for my life and explained
further the purpose of the exit visa and my delay. She said that I was
saved because my name was not found on the "black list." The black
list contained the names of those whom the state considered to be
dangerous, anti-government subversives. So, while we were waiting
patiently and wondering what was going on, government officials were
carefully scrutinizing the list (and even making phone calls) to find out
everything about my past and present activities. I later would find out
that had my name been on the list, for whatever reason, true or untrue,
I would have been immediately arrested, and in all likelihood would
have "disappeared" and been killed. We would quickly realize that this
was only the beginning of Liberia's problems.

In less than half an hour our passports were ready. The lady handed
the passports to us, but she declined our offer for lunch. Instead, she
requested that we simply provide her with some money for her lunch
so that we could leave as quickly as possible, which we gladly did.
She then advised us to leave immediately! Since our entire family was
leaving, the security boss was still suspicious of me and this woman
was afraid that someone might call in with new information at any
moment. After that exchange, we left the country the next day without
even waiting to obtain the necessary entry visas for Kenya.

When we arrived at the Kenyan International Airport, we were
taken into the security room and were questioned as to why we came
into Kenya without the necessary visas. I explained that we did not
know we needed to find a Kenyan visa issuing office in Monrovia since
we lived outside of the city. One of the immigration officers offered to
help me fill out all the documents, but I had to pay him $100 for each
visa. I accepted the offer since I didn't really feel that I had any choice.
We had only $600 on hand and gave him $500, which left us with
$100 to live on until our scholarship money arrived from Britain. The

immigration officers did help us by making a phone call to NEGST, and the school van came and picked us up. Our new life in Nairobi, Kenya had begun, and the Lord had delivered us from a dangerous situation in Liberia just in time.

At that time, the primary student housing on the NEGST campus were buildings from an old chicken farm. The farm had been bought from a European farmer that settled there during the colonial era when the British controlled Kenya. The actual chicken barns were slightly renovated and were being used by students as dormitories. We were given two rooms, one for my wife and me, and the other for our three children.

There was no personal kitchen. All students and their families ate in the cafeteria and the food was primarily what East Africans ate. Kenyans live on plantain and water grains (wheat, millet, etc.) whereas Liberians depended heavily on rice. Our children had a very difficult time adjusting to the food. They wanted rice so much that we had to purchase rice from the local market. Rice was very expensive since it was provided mainly for foreigners. In less than a month, we had run out of money and the scholarship funding had not arrived yet. To help us survive, the school offered to give us small monthly stipends until the scholarship money arrived. We went from September to December with no sign of any funds coming from Britain.

By December, Yah was sick almost every day, throwing up, not being able to hold down any food. Even the smell of cooking oil would upset her stomach. Finally, we realized that she was pregnant with Benjamin, our fourth child. Since Yah was ill throughout the pregnancy, I became a mother, a full-time student, and a father! When the time came for Yah to deliver, she experienced some complications and was rushed to a private hospital and had surgery. Ben was born on May 6, 1989. When she was discharged, we received a bill for more than $600. In Kenyan currency, it amounted to 13,000 Kenya shillings (Kshs). Once again, the school came to our aid and gave us a hospitality grant to clear the bills and encouraged me to concentrate on my studies.

After a while we took Ben to the hospital for circumcision, but he was diagnosed with a hernia and had to have surgery. At this time, the scholarship stipend had come in and we had some funds on hand to take care of the bills. However, when the bills were paid, we had very little to live on. To stretch our money, we adjusted to eating rice only once or twice a week and supplemented it with the Kenyan diet. But, we almost lost our older daughter Lily due to this drastic adjustment in eating habits. She constantly refused to eat what was put before her. We did not realize how serious her food adjustment problems were or how malnourished she was becoming.

One morning, I went into their room to awaken the children and get them ready for school. When I attempted to get Lily up, she started screaming. I realized that her body was very weak. She was so weak that she could not stand on her feet. At first, I thought she had gotten very sick in her sleep, but then she said, "Daddy, I am so very hungry." So, I rushed into the kitchen and brought some cold water and some pieces of bread. After she ate I put her back into bed and I took the other children to school. I then began to search for food that she would eat since I did not have the money to purchase any. There was an Australian student who was serving as a doctor for the campus at the time, so I went over to his apartment to see if I could borrow some money for rice. He gave me $20. I purchased some rice and prepared it for Lily.

When I went to pay back the loan, he asked me to sit down and we began a conversation. Before the end of our conversation, I noticed a really nice Canon K-1000 camera on his table; it even had a zoom lens. I asked why he had the camera, and he explained that he really did not have a use for it. He said he would like to sell it if he could find a buyer. I told him I would like to buy the camera to start a photography business, but there was one problem: I did not know how to use a camera! So he said he would teach me. He offered to sell me the camera for $400 on a payment plan. After he had taught me a few basic things, I set out to start my photography business on campus. My first clients were mothers of small children who wanted pictures of their children's birthday parties. I went from apartment to apartment to announce my new business venture and began to receive calls from several mothers as other mothers began to display my pictures in their homes.

I also found a place in Nairobi that would print them. Then the seminary itself became my second most important customer. One day, the principal called me and asked if I could take some pictures of special short-term guests of the seminary during their meetings and while they were enjoying special occasions. Having the seminary as a major customer, I was able to quickly pay off my camera. I was becoming more and more the "professional photographer" on campus. I was the photographer for the seminary's special events and would print the photos, place them in albums and submit my invoices. In a few days I would receive my payment in full. The photography business was now the financial means to our having adequate meals seven days a week. It also allowed us to save some money and buy small items for the children. In addition to photographing children and seminary events, I also photographed students at graduations and weddings. I charged very low rates as most of the students, like me, did not have much money.

I stayed in this business until the day I graduated in June of 1991. I received a Master of Divinity in Pastoral Studies from NEGST and was anxious to put my new training to work. I also wanted to visit my family in Liberia, but this would not be so easy, as I was soon to find out.

NEGST also offered classes for the wives, giving them language training in English as well as classes in knitting and baking. These gave Yah skills she would later use to help support the family.

Sei and Dr. Taylor –Pearce   **Sei and Yah at NEGST**
NEGST President

As a student at NEGST, I saw that all of us students could be used to advance God's kingdom. Some of the students, before graduating, were already serving as teaching assistants in the theological program as well as in the NEGST ladies program. Those who proved to be skillful teachers were sent or encouraged to further their training abroad in America or in the United Kingdom to perfect their skills. Furthermore, some of these students who studied abroad were offered a place on the teaching staff.

The NEGST faculty members firmly believed that each student was a vital part of God's bigger plan. They focused on developing to the fullest each individual man and woman. Each faculty member purposefully took several students under their wing and mentored them. During my time at NEGST, I served with Dr. Samuel Ngewa in an Africa Inland Church. In that church I led a prayer and Bible study and occasionally preached.

Some schools in Africa limit their student enrollment only to those in their denomination. Many seminaries or Bible colleges in Africa would never give their students recommendations for further study in America or Europe. They believed such students would not return to fulfill the institution's mission. NESGT, on the other hand, has never placed any restrictions on educational limits of the student. They encouraged students to go as far as possible in their education, and then, as the Lord led them, to return and invest back in NEGST, their home country, denomination or find their calling in another country. The calling might be in the church, in education, in government or even some area of business.

So, when a student leaves NEGST, they always feel that they have a higher role to play in the kingdom of God. Students are still always encouraged to come back as faculty, either to teach a course or seminar or as even more permanent staff. Those who come back as faculty are given full responsibility and respect to serve at NEGST. NEGST does not have a "them" (indigenous or national) vs. "us" (foreign experts) mentality. As I have thought about the best way to serve the people of Liberia, I have kept these attitudes and concepts with me over the years. (Note: NEGST changed its name in 2009 to Africa International University.)

Buors added Ben at NEGST   **NEGST Graduation**

*   *   *   *   *   *   *   *   *   *   *   *

Liberian Civil War

While I was studying in Nairobi, I had no idea that the problems in Liberia had become a bloody civil war. On December 24, 1989, we received the first news that a group of men, referred to as "Rebels," and who had been trained in Libya, crossed over into Liberia through Nimba County and attacked the Liberian government. At first, President Samuel Doe assured all of the citizens that he had dispatched troops to protect the borders and that everything would soon return to normal.

The next day, we heard different news on the BBC. Charles Taylor, a rebel leader, identified himself as the head of the "National Patriotic Front" and that he was responding to the cry of the people to deliver them from the tyranny of a military dictator who was the President. Taylor said that he would come to the aid of the people.

I began to get calls from several Liberian students who were in Nairobi, as well as calls from friends in Liberia. At first, we thought the Western media was blowing the news out of proportion. However, after a few weeks, the rebels were rapidly advancing and we received news they were recruiting more young men. Daily, we were hearing the stories of the rebels capturing or re-capturing towns and villages. We also heard the disturbing news that the government soldiers were carrying out reprisals against civilians whom they had suspected of harboring rebels.

Then, on March 12, 1990, I received bad news that devastated me. Early that morning, at around 3:00 a.m., our village had been burned to the ground and hundreds of the villagers had been killed or wounded. I would never have believed this to be possible! I was stunned. The next day I drove into Nairobi to find the International Red Cross office. I met a lady there that took down my family information. She promised to get back to me about their status and would find out if anyone from my family had survived the attack. But no news arrived. We waited anxiously for about three months. When we finally got the news, it was not good; indeed the village had been completely wiped off the map, and my father, Chief Buor, had been killed! My mother had fled, but had a broken wrist from a fall. She and the remnant of the village were hiding in the forest in the foothills near the mountain.

My mother's situation was critical because no one was sure that she would survive if she got an infection. Few medical facilities existed anywhere in Liberia, and it was impossible to get her to a neighboring country. Our family was not alone. Many of the Liberian students were also receiving similarly depressing news about their loved ones. Many people just disappeared; others were wounded and many died in the conflicts.

Due to my mother's condition, I decided that my family and I would return to Liberia right after graduation, and in 1991 we headed for Liberia. I made a final request to my scholarship sponsors asking them if they could help us purchase tickets to return to Liberia. My request was granted.

The flight was scheduled from Nairobi to Monrovia, Liberia, but instead we landed in the Ivory Coast, not as visitors, but as refugees. Ivory Coast was flooded with thousands of Liberian refugees. They were displaced in the streets of Abidjan and thousands more were streaming in each day from the border regions. Immediately, we became refugees.

Our friends could not understand why we would risk returning to Liberia only to become refugees like them! After a while, I began to wonder, too, but I desperately wanted news about my family and village. I made an attempt to visit the border hoping to find my mother and bring her with us, but that was far too risky and dangerous. Several rebel informers positioned themselves at the border to recruit members, both voluntarily and involuntarily, and they cautiously and suspiciously looked at anyone that wanted to enter Liberia.

Three weeks speedily passed. The days were becoming dreadful and there was little food available. Some refugee friends were still questioning our wisdom in returning. They, however, were also friendly and brought us some food since they had become experienced in locating food relief stations.

Chapter 6   Gambia, Here We Come!

Although I had made an unwise decision to try to return home to Liberia, God was faithful indeed! One day, I received a message from a refugee friend that a missionary in the city was looking for me and that I should try to contact him. The next morning I traveled about 20 miles to the missionary guest house. Upon arrival I was given a note about job offers in the nations of Ghana and Gambia. In Ghana I could teach in a Bible College. In Gambia I was offered a job as a missionary and senior pastor with the responsibility of training national leaders and doing evangelism among the Muslim populace. About 95% of Gambia's population of one million people are Muslim. During my seminary time I had taken courses in Islam and Muslim Evangelism and this training gave me the confidence, with God's leading, to accept the position in Gambia.

So it was that, while in Gambia, I served as a missionary/pastor and Bible school instructor with Worldwide Evangelization for Christ International (WEC) and the Evangelical Church of Gambia. We had the privilege of ministering in a cross-cultural setting. Several African nationalities, as well as Europeans and Australians, were represented in the congregation. It was both a humbling experience and a blessing from God to be used in developing and growing this congregation which was in great need of leadership. Below summarizes our time there.

Our family flew from Abidjan to the nation of Gambia. Upon arrival at the Banjul Airport we were met by Pastor Modou Sanneh and Shirley Strong. Pastor Modou, the President of the Evangelical Church of Gambia, was a native of Gambia and had a Muslim background. Shirley, the WEC International field director, was a native of Australia and was the leader of all WEC missionaries serving in Gambia. From the Banjul Airport we were driven through the city of Banjul and on to Serrekunda, ten miles from the capital city. From there we were taken to a very old building which had been fixed up to be our home. The building had three bedrooms and the floors were bare cement. There was no indoor toilet or kitchen - everything was located outside! But, we knew that this would be far better than living in a refugee camp!

Besides the house, there was another building in the same vicinity that was being used for discipleship classes and other activities. We were given a week to settle in before starting the ministry in Gambia.

Buors with Associate Pastor and Wife

The first week passed by quickly. Pastor Modou came to see us and show us around. We began with the "German Clinic," a small medical clinic built in the 1970's by some German missionaries. The clinic had ceased to function because the missionaries had returned home and there was no one equipped to run it. It was then that Modou informed me that this old medical clinic would be my church building. Across from the clinic a Mosque was nearly finished. When completed, the Mosque would hold about 75 to 150 people. After viewing the clinic, Modou took me to meet a Korean missionary that was part of the missionary team. Bin Ko Yu was really zealous about evangelism and making disciples. Every Sunday he went around the community gathering young people and bringing them to the Church. We visited several missionaries and prominent people, and everyone was excited to meet me.

On the second Sunday, Modou and Shirley took me to the German clinic and introduced me as the senior pastor. Thus began my ministry to this small congregation of 15 to 20 people that was called Omega

Church. There were also several missionaries who came for my inaugural sermon and to assure me of their support and prayers. Modou and
Shirley explained my responsibilities, which included care of the current congregation, but they also placed a strong emphasis on evangelizing and leadership development. From that day forward, I began my
ministry at the church in Gambia. I spent my first entire night planning for the ministry and went through my seminary notes on evangelizing Muslims. I started preaching and giving Bible studies. After a few
weeks we set up a leadership team which included elders and deacons,
and a financial committee. Things were beginning to come together at
Omega Church.

Although I was invited by the broader Gambia Evangelical Church,
the local congregation was actually responsible for my salary which was
set at 1,500 dalasis a month, the equivalent of $75 USD. By the end of
the first month there was not enough to pay me what they had planned
so I accepted a half-salary for about three months. Month after month
the church membership grew through our discipleship program where
many believers were excited about maturing in their faith. I held a
weekend seminar about giving, tithing and stewardship, and leadership responsibilities. After the seminar, our financial position radically
changed. Since the giving had increased, the Church now had enough
money to pay me and soon thereafter we decided to extend support to
President Modou's office and to other local evangelists as well.

The Omega Church began to draw more professional workers
among the foreign nationals and also from the American embassy in
Gambia which was less than a mile away from the church. As we grew,
we also delegated responsibilities to many mature and professional
members of our Church. We also attracted more Gambian nationals
to the worship service every week and the number of young people
increased. As the first year of ministry ended (1991) with great suc-
cess, we began the second year with great expectations of both growing
the local church as well as extending the outreach ministry to villages
beyond the city.

Midway into 1992 some of the youth members of Omega Church
came in with a young boy and introduced him to me as Tamba. Tamba
was about 11 or 12 years old. Our youth leader explained that Tamba

was a national of Sierra Leone and his village had been attacked and burned down by rebels and he just narrowly escaped! Tamba explained that he was not sure if his parents had survived. My wife provided food for the little boy and we let him sleep in our home that night.

The next morning we gave him some breakfast, but he was a little hesitant to eat. We were not exactly sure why he would not eat. Later on, when other scenarios began to unfold, we understood what the problem was. After two nights of caring for him, I decided to take him to the International Red Cross office in order to have him registered as a refugee. The office told me to leave him there for few hours for screening and they would call me when the processing was complete. About three hours later, I got a call from the office and, to my surprise, they said that the boy had confessed that he was in fact a rebel fighter who had narrowly escaped from a government ambush. His registration was completed and we brought him home. I called a meeting with our leaders to discuss how we should handle this very delicate issue.

We were debating whether or not we should surrender him to the police, give him over to the Red Cross, or just ask him to leave. The boy was willing to leave on his own and find a place to stay. So we allowed him to leave voluntarily. But after about three days he was picked up by the state security and he was traced to our church.

One morning about 9:00 a.m., five top-level presidential plain clothes security officers came to the church office and summoned me to go with them immediately for questioning. The men questioned me until about 4:30 p.m. They had sworn statements that, according to them, had come from Tamba. In the document, the little boy had confessed that he was one of 150 spies sent to Gambia with the intention of overthrowing the government. I was being questioned for harboring a spy. The case was especially critical since I was a national of Liberia and Charles Taylor, the rebel leader attacking the Liberian government, had well-known plans that he would like to overthrow governments in other West African countries. I was no doubt viewed as a possible rebel agent myself!

By 4:30 p.m., I had given my own statement and was free to return to my house. However, I was not to talk to anyone and I was not to leave my house. In a sense, I was under house arrest. When I returned home I explained to Yah exactly what had happened. She had been very worried and was unable to contact me to find out exactly what was going on.

At about 5:30 p.m. a group of presidential guards, well-equipped with AK 47 rifles, surrounded our house. Three entered the house and presented a search warrant. They began to search the house, turning everything upside down. Yah and I were very anxious, not knowing what they were looking for or what they would do next. They found nothing they wanted except the Canon camera which I had brought from Nairobi. In it were some undeveloped pictures I had taken on the way to Serrekunda and of other villages I had traveled through. I also had three new rolls of film.

When the search ended, they had confiscated my camera and film. The soldiers asked me to go with them and I was quickly put into their car. My children, after they came home from school and heard the story, and Yah began to weep. They assumed that they would never see me again. I was taken to one of the police stations and put in a cell with two other men. I was under tight security. At about midnight I asked the guard if I could call my wife and just let her know that I was still alive.

The guard was reluctant to accommodate me due to the nature of the charges and they were suspicious that I might be planning some escape plan. But after some time he allowed my request. Yah, meanwhile, had informed the church leaders of my arrest and prayed with our children that the Lord would protect me and bring me back to them safely. I called my wife and informed her that I was fine and that she should encourage the children to go to sleep since they were up as well worrying about me. She told me that the boys were refusing to go to bed unless they saw me. I told her I was not far from them and should be back any time and that they should go to bed.

The next morning the children were surprised to find that Yah had their breakfast ready and planned for them to go to school like any other school day. She reminded them that they had prayed for me and there was nothing they could accomplish anyway by staying home. She told them I would be most pleased if I knew they were at school and studying. I spent about three days in a cell and decided to begin fasting immediately. Each day some of the prisoners' families would bring food, but I refused to eat until I heard from God exactly what my fate would be as well as the future for my family. On the fourth day I had the opportunity to call my wife and let her know where I was imprisoned.

She informed our Church leaders. In the following days several members of our congregation and all the missionaries came to the police station. Yah brought me some great food at which time I broke my fast. Joyce, one of the ladies in our congregation, was an attorney and her father was also an attorney. Joyce vowed to make the arrest public before it was too late. She checked with a few other heads of security and was told the case was in the hands of the Presidential Security. Finally, the head of the Presidential Security agreed to release me on bond if there were Gambians that would sign a statement attesting to my character. More than ten Gambians showed up and surrendered their Gambian passports as a guarantee. That night my release was granted, but I was told to report to the police station daily. I reported to the police station daily for about a month and every time I was escorted by several of our leaders and missionaries. The daily reporting was eventually reduced to once a week and then to once a month. I continued with this inspection and questioning until I finally got a call informing me that I did not need to report anymore. I was not, however, allowed to go outside of the country unless I obtained permission.

One day a few of the prison guards came to visit me at my house in their plain clothes. We offered them local tea and food and had some great conversation. I encouraged them about their work and thanked them for taking good care of me. I also expressed appreciation for their high views of God and the Koran. I mentioned the Koran because when I was taken to prison, every office had on display a large size Koran. I am not sure if this prominent display meant they even read it at all; however, it was clear that they placed a high value on the Koran. I also admired these prison guards because I was very sure that, had this case occurred in Liberia, I would have been tortured and killed immediately upon my arrest. But these Gambian police and Presidential Security guards never once hurt me and never even insulted me. I began to share Christ with these men, and they came to visit me over and over again.

After several months had passed, I asked one of my guard friends to give me the phone number for the head of the Presidential guard and this he did.

I prayed and then called Mr. Dabou, the chief of Presidential Security. The phone call went directly to his desk. I explained that the reason for my call was that during the search of my house my camera was taken. I let him know that the camera meant a great deal to me and my family. I told him that he could have the film, but I really needed the camera back. The security chief apologized. He instructed me to go to the police commander to get my camera back but he also told me to leave the exposed film since they were still investigating the pictures. I quickly ran to the police station and went to the police commander's office. The camera was there. It had been locked up in a safe. I sat in the commander's office and had several minutes of conversation with him, thanked him for his great work, and then left. Finally the case slowly died down and the passports for my bond were returned to their owners. I experienced God's love through His people that risked their own welfare and security so that I might live.

After experiencing imprisonment and ongoing questioning from the local authorities, my faith in God was ever deepened. I continued the work of teaching, evangelizing, and developing local church leadership. I knew that God wanted me to develop local leaders to prepare them to eventually take on the main roles in the ministry. As a result of this conviction and my role in developing people, Yah and I and the other leaders ordained a young Gambian man and his wife to take over leadership of the ministry. Matthias was working full time with Campus Crusade and his wife Ayeisha was an administrative assistant to a human rights organization. Matthias and Ayeisha's son, Ryan, was the first baby we dedicated about three months after our arrival at Omega Church.

*   *   *   *   *   *   *   *   *   *   *   *

The second year of ministry ended and we began 1993, again with great excitement. We felt that we had finally settled into everyday life in Gambia. One day I began to go through some of the items I had brought from NEGST. Suddenly, I came across a list of five institutions that a visiting professor had given to me. Often the professor would ask me what I was planning to do after completing my schooling at NEGST. I replied that I would like to do a Master's program somewhere in Asia.   He gave me the list of colleges and encouraged me to pursue my advanced studies in his country, America. I then remembered the movie about Sammy Morris and how the missionaries told him that he needed training from an American college. I had taken that list and placed it in my file folder and never got back to it until that day.

Yah and I began to talk and pray about the possibility of my going to America for a year to study. That night, I started filling out applications to all the schools. Eventually all the schools responded. Four schools replied that they did not have a scholarship program for international students. The fifth institution replied that they had just given out all of the remaining scholarships for 1993, but they did encourage me to apply in 1994. They explained that I needed to still take the TOEFL admittance exam which would test my ability to read and write English. I talked to a few of my Gambian friends and I began to study for the test. I scored a 575, which was 25 points higher than the 550 score required by the school. The exam coordinators submitted my score to Western Theological Seminary in Holland, Michigan.

I waited for about three months and finally the reply arrived. The program director, Dr. George Hunsberger, gave me admission, 100% scholarship, $150 monthly stipend, and full health insurance! I took the document to the American Embassy and I was granted a visa to travel to America to pursue a Master of Theology degree.

This was a sign to me that God had further educational blessings and plans for my life. I began preparing a local Gambian to take my place as the pastor to the congregation. The adventure was continuing! There was one other important prayer, though, that I needed God to answer.

Chapter 7   The Seed is Planted: God's Vision for Liberia

I wanted to see my mother in Liberia before I made any other trip. I asked God in prayer if he would protect me and permit such a thing to happen. I received an answer. The Lord made it clear that he would protect me. I called our congregation and church elders and informed them of my decision to return to Liberia to see my mother before leaving for America. Everyone concluded, however, that this was a bad idea.

Our first decision to go back to Liberia had been after I had finished my study in Kenya. That decision had resulted in our only getting as far as Abidjan. God had intervened and I had accepted this hindrance as His will and the results were good. Now, once again, I was trying to return to Liberia to see my mother. This time I was leaving my family in a strange land. The risk was very real as rebels were everywhere. They were raping, plundering, and executing whomever they willed. After everyone, including my wife, failed to convince me not to make the trip, I purchased a ticket and took off for Abidjan.

I landed in Abidjan without alerting anyone I was there and took a bus to one of the border towns. After an all night ride I arrived about 5:30 a.m. the next morning. I spoke to a couple of refugees there and they all warned me about the dangers of going into Liberia, but I was not deterred in any way. I got rid of all of my possessions and clothing, and dressed like any one of the people living in the region. I then started walking on the road with the few people who were going into Liberia. Some of the people were genuine travelers, but some were rebels or government informers spying on anyone that was entering the country. They were also traveling back and forth to kidnap those they perceived as their enemies. This was a highly dangerous situation and I knew it, but I was driven to see my mother. I knew somehow that God would protect me.

I was blessed to find some special escorts that had been my former students and previous co-workers. They offered to be my guide on my journey. At first, I was afraid that they might betray me, because I didn't know which side they were supporting! Some of my escorts told me point blank that they were among the rebel fighters, but would take me through without harm. I finally accepted the offer and in return told them that I would take care of their food and other travel expenses. Once we started, the group divided into four teams. One group went ahead to watch out for any danger while another stayed close to me. Two others groups followed behind us at a distance. At the first check-point we came face-to-face with hundreds of rebels. Some were there waiting for training while others were waiting for orders from their leaders. I had a small suitcase which was being handled by one of my escorts. The luggage was checked and cleared and we were then able to proceed through the gate.

Right after we passed the gate we saw an open pickup truck. We saw it as a quick way to further our journey. The driver was one of the rebel commanders, and he had a few soldiers with him. One of my escorts went to him and explained that we were on our way to a Christian conference and asked for a lift. My escort offered to pay the commander for gas. The commander said ok, and we got into the pickup and went several miles.

Suddenly, he stopped and announced that he had received a call to return immediately to the war front. So we got out, trekked on, and arrived in a little town called Bahn. Bahn had previously fallen into the hands of government soldiers with the help of the Mandingos (a Muslim ethnic group), but had just been recaptured by the rebels in one of the many battles between government soldiers and the rebels. The Mandingo residents of the town were completely wiped out along with several hundred government soldiers. Sadly, this was very common in those days of civil war.

For fear of government reprisals, we bypassed the town, as we did not want to be mistaken for spies. Soon we arrived at an old missionary station. There were nearly 50 Christian leaders gathered there to pray and to hold a leadership meeting. When they found out I was a pastor, they asked me if I would preach. I said, "yes" and I agreed to stay on for a couple of days. I took my text from the book of Acts (Chap. 26:1-6) and preached about the time the Apostle Paul been bitten by a deadly snake. The Islanders were watching for Paul to swell up and die, but

God protected him from any harm. I encouraged them to stand firm in their faith and declared that God would protect them in the midst of the anarchy.

When I concluded the message, a group of the senior elders and leaders stood up and publicly asked me to help with leadership development among the indigenous Christians. They specifically begged me to develop a Bible College to train courageous leaders for our nation and the Church of Jesus Christ. (Some of the leaders that attended that meeting are presently in America, and one of them is now President of the ULICAF Board of Trustees.) I pondered the request and kept it in my heart only since I did not have the means to fulfill such a dream, no matter what my passion and vision were. I never forgot, though, that exhortation and encouraging word!

The next day I bid them farewell and took off again to find my mother. Based on my experiences in Africa as a student, and later as a Christian leader, I began to see a need for transforming leadership patterned after New Testament biblical principles. I planned, therefore, to pursue advanced studies that would hopefully allow me to develop strategies for discipling both young and old people, using the Bible as the main handbook and authority along with other discipleship books as additional valuable resources. I was beginning to get some glimpses of my calling as a Christian educator.

It is true that the African Church is growing by leaps and bounds, but one often fails to find the depth that will sustain such growth in the next generation. The future leaders are on the ground right now in Liberia waiting for further training. I give great thanks to the many faithful missionaries that have cultivated the existing field of workers. I believe that, like the second generation of New Testament disciples of Jesus, I am now being sent to reap what others have labored over for many years. As Jesus indeed said, "The harvest is plenty but the laborers are few (John 4:38)."

Because of the civil war in Liberia, many Christian leaders were killed. The social structure of the country was destroyed and the bitter conflict left many tribes disillusioned and with no faith in reconciliation – even with former neighbor villages. I wanted to acquire an advanced education to enable me to play a vital role in rebuilding our country. The entire leadership of my region (Nimba County) in Liberia was wiped out at the outset of the civil war. Shortly before my departure for the United States, the leadership of my church had a conference to discuss the future of Liberia. The need for advanced theological training was one of the issues brought up at this conference.

God works in mysterious ways. I believe God brought me to these men and women of God to help them, while at the same time my faith was built up by hearing the stories of the severe trials of their faith. We were a gift from God to each other. It would be many years before I would have a chance to practically design and develop this "dream" of a Christian college, but the seed for LICC was planted right there in a small meeting of the Christian faithful in Liberia!

After leaving the church leaders, I was still about 55 miles away from my village. I made the trip uneventfully while I tried to prepare my mind and heart to face the tragedy of what happened in my village. There was no way I could have known how my heart would be torn to pieces when I arrived.

When I came to our village, I could find no sign of human life. Nothing existed but a forest! Not a single building or structure of any kind was evident. Had you not lived there prior to the civil war, you would have never imagined that anyone ever lived there at all and that it once was a vibrant village the home of many loving families.

I was in complete shock. The buildings that had been there before were non-existent. There was absolutely nothing. I don't yet know how to describe the feelings. I had received a list of people who had died and I went through the village area looking for any sign that these people even existed. For example I tried to find the location of my father's house. It was gone. I then thought about the bodies. Were they given a decent burial? What happened to my father? He was blind and the house had been set on fire. Was he buried or left as a charred corpse to be torn apart by animals?

I wandered from place to place looking at the location of each house (as close as I could tell) and wondered where each family member was located. What had happened to the families of my closest friends? Who was dead and who was alive?

I experienced a deep sense of loss which was like a gaping hole in my heart. The senselessness of the killing and destruction was overwhelming. I could not force myself to move on until I had thought about and mourned for many family members and friends. My escorts understood and they waited patiently for me to grieve.

Eventually, my escorts led me on a bush path to find the place where the remnants of the village were hiding. It took us about three hours before we finally arrived at the foothills of a mountainous area. My escorts went ahead to make sure that it was the right place, and behold it was! I found my mother there! After seeing the site of my former home village you can imagine how joyful I was to see her. She was weak but managed to rise up and embrace me. She began to dance around. She even asked me to sit on her lap, but I joked that I would crush her since I was not her baby anymore. She then asked about Yah and the children and about Benjamin whom she had never seen. Ben was born in Nairobi and had never been home to our village.

I had planned to stay in the village for at least two weeks before returning, but the elders told me absolutely not to do so. Then my mother called a few of the older folks who advised me to leave because my life was in danger and I would be endangering their lives as well. They also indicated that the wickedness in the land was increasing. She said that I should return home to Gambia to take care of her grandchildren. She also reminded me that before I left for Kenya, I had brought in some white people (missionaries) and that we had preached and assured the people about heaven and of living together with Jesus as one family. She was referring to our past messages about Jesus our Savior and eternal life in heaven with God where there will be no more wars and, most importantly, no more separation of families.

Then she said that if she is a Christian and dies, she will be with Jesus. "We will all one day be together with Jesus," she said. She further told me, "From what you preached, there is no need for you to be afraid for me or to risk your life by leaving Yah and the children in another country." I was overjoyed to know that she was truly a believer and was growing so strong in her faith. I stayed only a week there and decided to make my way out again.

I wanted to look at other parts of the country as I made my way out of Liberia. One of Charles Taylor's rebel bases was nearby and one of the commanders heard about me and came to meet me at another village. He desired to serve as my escort. The next day we started on a journey to Ganta. Between Ganta and Monrovia is the city of Gbarnga in Bong County which was the headquarters for Charles Taylor. The commander and I got in an open-backed pickup truck with food supplies purchased for the trip. At each rebel checkpoint, the commander got down and everyone saluted him. He then let the guards know that there was a special official with him who was looking at "investment opportunities." He then gave out food, cigarettes, and other items to the guards and we went on our way.

Upon our arrival in Gbarnga, we came to a notorious checkpoint where hundreds of civilians had been killed. When we arrived, the rebels came out and checked for weapons. Instantly, when one of the young men saw me, he began to shout in the air. A wave of fear swept through us; however, this young man had been in one of the mission schools when I was a principal and was just excited to see me! What a relief that was! In his joy he asked me to come to meet his gate commander. I reluctantly followed him about 500 feet into the bush behind the gate to meet the gate commander. I tried to shake hands with the man, but the commander was unable to stand because he was under the influence of drugs. Anxious not to upset him, I attempted to give him some money but he refused very forcefully.

Later, the commander I was with explained that if the gate commander had accepted the gift and it turned out that I was a spy, all of them would be executed immediately. After meeting the gate commander, we crossed the gate and entered the city of Gbarnga. There were rebel soldiers everywhere. Later, when we were ready to leave, I asked the commander if we could enter Monrovia, but he warned me against going there. Instead, we returned to the border. The next day I said goodbye to all my escorts and gave them everything I had as a token of my appreciation for the risk they personally had taken in helping me. I then crossed the border into the Ivory Coast. Once there, I caught a bus back to the city of Abidjan where I made a phone call to Gambia to let Yah and the church know that the Lord had protected me and I was on my way home back to them. Finally, I got on the flight to Gambia where I was met by Yah and the children, all of whom were rejoicing along with the church.

The Lord had truly been answering our prayers. I had received a scholarship to attend advanced studies in America, had seen my mother, and had witnessed firsthand Liberia's devastation. Additionally, I had been commissioned by the elders to develop sound biblical leadership for the church and the nation. I scheduled my departure for America for September of 1994.

Chapter 8   Another School, Another Culture

The Bible teaches a principle that "man may have his own plan" but God has His plan and the implementation. Our idea of how "the plan" should work out is often very different from God's plan, and the ways in which He brings His purposes to pass! Once again I would find this out, as I prepared to depart for America for my future studies.

I began preparations for departure for the United States as soon as I returned to Gambia. Yah and I had discussed that I should complete my studies within a year and return to them in Gambia before we all together return to Liberia.

Then one morning we heard news that the Gambian soldiers that were serving alongside the West African intervention forces in Liberia were returning home. While this news in itself wasn't alarming, in the next few days tension began to rise as news spread that the returning soldiers were not getting their pay. Before their departure, the government had agreed to pay them when they returned, but now the government refused to fulfill its promise. The soldiers staged a demonstration demanding their pay. This was no ordinary demonstration. The demonstration started in the morning, but by noon it had turned into a military coup led by a new leader, Yaya Jameh, who was only about 28 years old. The incumbent president was escorted to a boat and an appeal was made to the British to allow him to be exiled to England.

The new leader suspended the constitution and closed down the airport so no flights could leave or enter. Thousands of tourists became stranded in the country and it took British government intervention to airlift all British citizens through specially chartered flights. There was also news that the unseated president was about to bring in troops from Senegal to restore the government. Any appearance of the impending stability that we Liberians had hoped for was brief.

At this point in time it appeared as if our original plans would be drastically altered. I could cancel the plan completely, move my family to Liberia or move back to Abidjan. Once again, the Lord led the way. I found a phone number for one of my former professors at Nairobi Evangelical Graduate School of Theology (NEGST), Toni Wilmot. He was one of the founding fathers of NEGST. I called Toni, who had returned to his homeland of Great Britain and explained what had happened to my plans. After some discussion, Toni promised to send me an affidavit of support and suggested I appeal to the British Consulate for a visa to go through England on my way to America. The fax came in the next day and I took it to the British consulate office. I had the advantage that I had already obtained an American visa. The British consulate knew that I was just going through England and they readily granted my request.

My next concern was leaving my family in the middle of the coup in Gambia. I talked this over with my wife and the children. Yah said to me, "I have prayed about this and God has shown me that you must go and I must stay here and be strong for the children. I am 100% sure this is what God wants." The children agreed that I should leave. I promised to make a way for them to come to America or that I would come back to Gambia in a year no matter what happened.

The following week I found a seat on the British Airways flight out of Gambia and left the country without any trouble. Toni picked me up from the Heathrow Airport in London and took me to his house in Sevenoaks, England. I stayed with Toni and his wife Eve for about two weeks and spent some time there speaking, by invitation, at several different churches. I boarded a flight for New York because I did not have enough money to fly directly to Holland, Michigan.

I also wanted to stop in New York because I had heard that Africans had lived in New York in the past and I just thought there was something special about New York. Lastly, a year before my coming to America, a young man from our church in Gambia was accepted at a University in New York and begged me to stop and see him if I was ever to visit the United States. I enjoyed my stay in New York with him. Then, I got on a Greyhound bus for Holland, Michigan.

I was on the bus to Holland, Michigan for almost two days and finally, late at night, I arrived at the bus station at 10:00 p.m. When the bus driver announced on the intercom that we had arrived at our destination, I looked through the bus window.

There were very few people waiting outside. I did see a lady standing there holding a poster that read, "Sei Buor, Welcome to Holland, Michigan." The lady holding the poster was Dawn Boelkins, Director of the Seminary's International Admission office. Dawn told me that my dormitory room was not ready, but she had arranged for me to stay in a Reformed Church mission guesthouse. I loaded all of my things into her car and was driven to the home where I would stay for a few days until my dorm room was readied.

When we arrived in the guesthouse, there was a handwritten note on the table addressed to me. The note read, "We have been waiting for you but sorry that we have to leave. Your friend Eugenia De Haas told us all about you and she wants you to be our friend. We will come by on Sunday morning to take you to our church." The note was signed "the Van Wylens."

I had first met Mrs. Eugenia De Haas at the Amsterdam 1986 Itinerant Evangelistic Conference. At that time she was the director of a neighborhood Bible study with its headquarters in America. One afternoon during the conference break period, I stopped by the booth where she was displaying her study materials. She asked where I was from and I told her Liberia. I explained that I was in my last year in Bible College and planned to be a pastor. She asked for my permission to record an interview with me for her husband back in America. I agreed and we did the recording. Before we departed she gave me her phone contact and mailing address in America. She also gave me a few of the study materials to start a student ministry.

Since then, Dr. and Mrs. De Haas have become my partners in the ministry of the gospel – true mentors, networkers and supporters. Prior to my coming to America, she had planned for me to stop in Orono, Maine to visit them, but Eugenia had some medical issues at the time and it did not work out. She referred me, however, to some good friends of hers who lived in Holland, Michigan, Dr. Gordon and Margaret Van Wylen. She and Margaret had attended Michigan State University together in the late 1940s. Margaret had been studying to be a medical doctor and Eugenia was preparing to be a nurse. During the course of their studies these two young students were connected through InterVarsity Christian Fellowship on campus and their friendship continued their entire life.

Between that Wednesday night and Sunday morning I anxiously waited to meet my first American friends and to experience my first worship time in America. Then, Sunday finally came and the Van Wylens arrived as promised in the letter. I was already dressed when the car came in the driveway and quickly went out to meet them. Both Margaret and Gordon got out and greeted me and we set off for church. We had some conversation on the way about my experience on the long flight from Africa and my thoughts about coming to America. Finally, we entered Christ Memorial Church. The building was huge and there were cars pulling in from everywhere. There were literally thousands of people walking through the doors. The building had one main entrance but it appeared like there were people entering almost everywhere in the building. What a contrast to my little church back in Africa. We made our way slowly to the door and Gordon held the door open for Margaret and me as we entered.

Once inside the building, I peered into the sanctuary and the pastor was just wrapping up the first service, so we waited at the coffee area for the second service to begin. One thing that caught my attention immediately was that I did not see any black people in the church; it was all white people! I became the only black attendee of the church.

Conversely, there are few white people in the African countryside. Most of the whites I knew were missionaries. So, all that we really knew about America was our positive experience with the missionaries (and now my new encounters with American television programs). The whites I knew were loving Christians who made personal sacrifices to share the gospel with us. They were a minority in Africa. When I got to Holland I found it was a completely white village! Later I was to learn there were a few black people on the outskirts of town. But I clearly saw that I was now in the minority. This was a great cultural shock! No blacks at all. I had not thought about this as a possibility, so it was quite an adjustment to me. The church had two services. The first one was a traditional service filled with older men and women. The second service was more informal with contemporary music and attracted many younger people.

When the first service ended, people began to go in several directions at once all over the building. Most of the people came to the coffee area and some went to the Sunday school classes of their choice. Most of the people that came to the coffee area would walk up to me and say

"Hi," and I replied by saying "Hello." Immediately, most would mention something about my accent and ask where I came from. I replied "Africa" or "Liberia." Some would end their questions there but others would ask a second question, "Where is Liberia?" I was frustrated in my explanations since no one seemed to know anything about Liberia or even Africa. Also, because of my deep accent and careless enunciation, I am afraid I probably confused them even more. Nonetheless, the atmosphere was very friendly as they smiled and welcomed me to their beautiful country and to their church.

The coffee time ended and the second service started. Everything was quite different and seemed spectacular to me. The order of worship was arranged perfectly, suggesting hours of preparation and planning. And everyone did his or her part just perfectly. The choir director was lively and very special. The "announcer" followed a very set schedule and kept the service moving along. Finally the preacher came. The minister was a tall man (about six feet tall) and distinguished looking. His message was special and spirit-filled. I loved his preaching style so much that I had no difficulty deciding that this would be my home church in America! When the preaching concluded, the preacher came out and my host introduced him to me as Tim Brown. Tim was very friendly and said to me, "you are a good man, welcome, and we love you." The pastor's friendliness and welcoming remarks confirmed my decision to settle in at this church in Holland, Michigan.

Even though I initially felt lonely at Christ Memorial Church, because I was so different looking, this feeling was quickly overcome by the preaching and the friendliness of the people. The pastor was down to earth. I was impressed by the way the pastor was preaching the Bible and this appealed to me very much.

After meeting the preacher, Gordon and Margaret took me out for lunch and finally drove me back to my guest apartment. The week quickly passed. Soon my dorm room was ready. I moved onto the Seminary campus two days before the international students' orientation, so I had two days to get settled in, enjoy my rest, reflect on my journey, and just try to make sense of all of my new experiences in America.

A day after my arrival on campus two other international students arrived, one from the Philippines and the other from Indonesia. We became friends almost immediately. On orientation day Dr. George Hunsberger appeared and introduced himself as the department head. I looked at my admission letter and previous letters and my memory was correct. The name was the same. I prayed for George and let God know that here stood my "miracle professor," the one whose single response so inspired me and gave me hope. He had in a way empowered me to obtain a visa from the American Embassy, and that got me into America! Other than that, I had no idea what kind of person Dr. Hunsberger would be, nor did he even know that he was someone so special in my life.

George's name even appeared on my class schedule. What a divine coincidence! He would be teaching my first theological and missions course at the school. I made a secret vow right then and there that I would make George proud of his decision to admit me to Western Theological Seminary. For me, that meant I would do everything I could to excel in all his classes. I would become one of the best students. A few other professors introduced themselves, but I don't remember much about them. I was thanking God silently for Dr. George Hunsberger's creating the opportunity for me to study here.

Perhaps, one might think after all I had gone through to get this far, that the rest would be easy, but that was not the case. There were many challenges that came with going to school in America.

I had attended the best schools that were available to me in Africa, but there were many differences. For example, from the very start of the course work, most of the professors required that all assignment papers be typed. That did not bother me as I had learned how to type on a typewriter and was very efficient and fast – or so I thought – and could type about 40 or 50 words per minute. The seminary, however, had no typewriters and very few computers. I had also never touched a computer prior to coming to America. Certainly, I didn't have one myself. So I would have to use the computer in the library that was available for all students. To manage this the library required students to sign on for two hours at a time and then let another student take their two-hour turn. Several times I became stuck or frustrated with my lack of computer skills. I sought the help of the librarian and, for that matter, anyone else in the library that I came in contact with that might know something about computers. In the end, I was able to do my thesis on a computer with a little help from our church secretary who properly formatted it for me.

Caring for my family was another major challenge. As a student one can expect to live with limited money, but a father has an obligation to provide for his family. My scholarship included a stipend of $150 which was enough to support me in America. I got adjusted easily to American food and ate most of the time in the cafeteria. However, I needed a little more to support my family back in Gambia. So I submitted a job application to the seminary and was hired as a custodian. My job responsibilities included mopping the seminary floor, taking out trash in all the offices, making coffee, and setting up classrooms. I was paid $5.25 per hour and the job required two hours in the morning and two hours in the evening. From Monday through Friday I left my apartment at 5:30 a.m. to get into the building to complete my tasks, after which I returned home to shower and get ready for class. I used the income from this job to help support my family in Gambia.

I should mention here the resourcefulness of my wife Yah. The Bible speaks in Proverbs (Chapter 31) of the "wife of noble character." When I think of that woman in Proverbs, I think she has nothing on Yah. While I was in Gambia we purchased a propane stove from the support we had received from the Church. With that stove Yah started a bread baking business. She faithfully baked and sold bread to both the local people and foreign missionaries in the city. When I left for Holland, Michigan, Yah continued the business to support the family. She and the four children were left there with her alone to adequately care for the family. That meant that she got up at 5:00 a.m. to start the first batch of bread, to carry water, and to do all the other chores to start the day. She had to take over the chores I had done as well as do all her own. She worked hard and earned enough to pay for the children's private school fees and to provide for their other needs.

Yah also put in much physical and creative effort to keep the spirits of the children up in order to not let them be sad or discouraged because I was not there. Until that time, they had always had both parents at home every day. Both of us had always been active in their lives. Yah would think of fun things for them to do together. Often she would run and play with them and challenge them to try to catch her. She read my letters aloud to the children and helped them write letters to me. She was also strict and required them to complete their home-work, excel in school, and still finish all of their chores at home!

A couple of times she took a little extra money she had made from the bread baking and purchased a chicken and cooked it on the open grill as a special treat. She saved money, however, for the future, and when she arrived in the United States she brought $1,000 (US money) with her to be used carefully in those first few months.

"While the children were in school," Yah relates, "I often walked to visit people from the church that were ill or lonely. God was very gracious to us during that time. He provided many friends for the children and for me also. He provided for all of our needs. It was a precious time for me with our children. I learned a lot about myself and I learned to do a lot of things I would never have considered in other circumstances."

One of the most exciting days for the children came when I took the money I earned as a custodian in the United States and purchased shoes for each child. I mailed those shoes to them. When they got home from school, Yah surprised them with that package for them to open. They still have fond memories of that day and those shoes!

Chapter 9   Complete Again

I continued attending Christ Memorial Church, a large congregation of about 4,000 members led by senior pastor Tim Brown. On one morning, he encouraged the congregation to participate in a discipleship program called, *Walk Through the Bible* (www.walkthru.org). I registered for the event. During the activities, the facilitator placed us into several small groups and Tim and I were placed in the same group. Our group ended up winning a prize for our knowledge of the Bible. When the program ended, Tim commented on my depth of knowledge of the Bible and expressed an interest in getting to know me. He asked me if I would be willing to help with setting up for weddings and special events. I agreed and several times came in to assist with directing traffic, setting up the rooms, or just spending time talking with him. He also asked me to preach during the evening service. Over the next two and a half years we developed a great, enduring friendship.

In seminary, my studies were progressing very well. When exam week arrived, I was focused on making good grades and so I studied all of the time. One night the phone rang and on the other end was the voice of Tim Brown asking me what I was doing. I explained that I was studying and having a difficult time concentrating because I was feeling lonely without my wife and children. I had been in America for almost six months and most of the news reports from Gambia were quite unsettling.

Tim asked me, "When do you want your family to come?"

I replied, "I don't know."

Tim repeated the same question, "When do you want them to come?"

Again, I said, "I don't know."

He asked another question, "How much will it cost for them to come?"

Again, I replied, "I don't know - maybe about $10,000." I really didn't know for sure.

Tim ended the conversation by saying that he would pray for my family and he said that if God wanted them to come, *He* would provide the $10,000 I needed. When the conversation concluded, I prayed and asked God to help me get my family to America, and then I continued on with my studies.

About two weeks after our conversation, I called Tim to see if he was still serious about praying for my family to come to America. He replied, "Yes." He also added that he had asked his associate pastor of congregational care, Rev. Dave Kool, to contact the seminary and find out the exact cost to bring my family to America. Pastor Dave and I then went to inquire at the seminary about all the details of bringing my family to America.

The next day Pastor Dave called and asked me to meet him at the seminary. We both went into the office of Dawn Boelkins, the Director of International Students. Dawn was the woman that picked me up from the bus station the day of my arrival. Dawn explained that the school's policy was to train students and send them back to their country to spread the gospel to their people. They were not in favor of bringing their families over to the United States since often the student stayed in America rather than going back to their homeland to train their people. She also estimated the cost to be far higher than I had imagined. Her costs included not only the plane fare, but also six months of apartment rent, health insurance, food, etc. She emphasized that this total cost was much higher than the school policy would approve. Dave explained that it was the Senior Pastor and the elders of the church that wanted to know the estimated expenses. She also said that since my family was not in any apparent danger in Gambia it would be difficult to obtain a travel visa from the American Embassy. I returned to my dormitory a little bit discouraged thinking that was the end of the case.

The next day Dawn said that she had faxed the American Embassy in Gambia to validate her opinion that my family was in no danger; however, the response came back saying that yes, indeed, my family was in very real danger! A military coup had taken place prior to my coming to the States and was followed by several other failed coups. The political setting was unstable at best and everyone feared that something worse than a coup could happen at any moment. The document further explained that my family was living close to the military barracks. This report changed Dawn's heart, and the seminary administrators began to support the idea of my family coming to join me. The president of the seminary, Dr. Dennis Voskuil, offered to personally pay for six-months rent when my family arrived. Others promised food and money. Dawn prepared the "Affidavit of Support" and very quickly the Embassy granted my family visas to come to America. Christ Memorial Church paid for the tickets. One other miracle also occurred prior to my family's arrival. The Seminary had a kitchen that fed the homeless and low-income individuals at noon every day. A handicapped lady came often to help give out soup. She had a hard time getting in and out of her car, and I would often assist her. On several occasions I went to her mobile home to cut her lawn. One day she asked me if I could come to speak to her ladies' Bible study at First Presbyterian Church in Holland. She was mostly interested in hearing about the wildlife in Africa; however, I ended up sharing about Christ, my personal testimony, and every day life in Africa. The following Saturday an older couple showed up at my door. The lady introduced her husband, Lewis Beem (Lou) and herself, Virginia. She said she had attended my previous talk and was blessed and so she brought her husband to personally meet me.

Lou was a harmonica player and offered to sing a special song for me. He sang a song having the lyrics, "Count your blessings, name them one by one, and see what God has done." Before they left, they presented me with a few bags of vegetables, apples and strawberries. Lou and Virginia Beem invited me to visit their home and also said that they had a second car that I could use any time for purchasing groceries and running other errands. Later, before my family's arrival, Lou and Virginia had been in Florida for the winter. Lou called his brother Leo and his wife Annie and asked them to go clean their house, pick up everything, and to then turn the key over to us when my family arrived so we could stay at their home. We lived in the Beems' home for about two-and-a-half months before moving to an apartment. Both Lou and Virginia have now gone to be with the Lord, but Leo and Annie still remain our special friends in Holland.

Finally, my family arrived from Gambia! Pastor Dave and I drove to Chicago to meet Yah and the four children at O'Hare International Airport on March 9, 1995. What an amazing answer to prayer!

At the Sunday worship our family received the warmest welcome from the congregation at Christ Memorial Church. There were gifts, smiles, praises and thanks to God from everyone we met. The local newspaper, The Holland Sentinel, carried the news of my family's arrival and our reunion. Tim Brown and his elders presented us to the congregation as their missionaries-in-residence. When the six-month lease on our rented house expired, Christ Memorial took over the financial responsibility, paying for our food and rent. Holland Christian High School granted 100% scholarships to all the children. When Priscilla, a lady in Christ Memorial's choir, could no longer safely drive due to age and health issues, she donated her car to our family. For a time, everyone in Holland talked about the arrival and reunion of my family. What an incredible welcome to America!

God continued to bless us. There are many blueberry and apple farms in Holland and the adjacent areas. One day, Lou and Virginia invited us to go pick blueberries, and so we took the whole family out to a nearby farm. The farm owner was excited to see us and expressed appreciation. We picked blueberries for ourselves but the farm owner refused to let us pay for any of it since we were their special guests.

Before we left, he offered us the opportunity to make some money if we were in the position to do so. He asked us if we would be interested in coming to the farm early in the morning to pick berries for him. We agreed, and the next morning Yah and I arrived at 6:00 a.m. without the children. We were paid $1.50 per each container we filled. By picking blueberries early in the morning, we could easily earn three hundred or more dollars in less than a week. Our children also agreed to come and pick out bad berries from the conveyer belt. In a short time we made enough extra cash that we were able to purchase little items such as bikes for our children.

When the blueberry season ended, Yah found a babysitting job with a professor at Hope College and I found a second job with Hope Church. I was responsible for washing all their communion cups and cleaning their kitchen every Monday morning. In return, the Church contributed $200 to my scholarship funds in the Seminary. I continued working at both the seminary and Hope church until I graduated in December, 1995.

While we were in Holland I found another friend. One day, when we were in the parking lot at Meijers, a woman with a baby started following us. Finally, she came up to us and asked us, "Are you from Haiti?"

We said, "No."

Then the woman, whose name was Amber, said, "Your accent sounded so familiar. We were missionaries in Haiti." She invited us to her home in Zeeland, near Holland, and we went there to visit them. Her husband, Phil Snyder, is a very down-to-earth man. He ended up being the first partner of our ministry (ULICAF).

Phil had a 501(C)(3), Glow Ministries International (GLOW), a tax-exempt ministry, and he volunteered to accept gifts for our ministry and issue appropriate receipts for our donors. Our friendship has continued to grow and they presently continue to support us financially. Whenever I go to Holland, I always plan a visit to their home.

Rev. Jack (known as Ben) and Lauretta Patterson are another special couple that came into our lives in Holland. They were prayer warriors and faithfully studied the Word of God. I first met Ben and Lauretta at Christ Memorial Church in Holland. Ben was a full-time chaplain at Hope College and came to Christ Memorial Church regularly to preach. My first encounter with Ben was after one of his sermons and before my family arrived. On this occasion I simply walked over to him during a coffee break to thank him for what I thought was one of his best expository messages. During our conversation, I realized that not only was he a good preacher, but he was also a prayer warrior.

Liberia was still experiencing brutal civil war and my wife and children were still trying to find a way to come to the United States. I sensed my need for prayer and that became the connection that led to a long-lasting friendship with Ben and Lauretta. We scheduled a weekly prayer time in their home. Lauretta, Ben's wife, their four children and two other ladies were in our first meeting. One of the ladies was Ben's assistant from Hope College and the other lady was from the Vineyard, a local church known for prayer and revival meetings. Ben was truly a student of the Bible. He not only memorized scripture verses but also had committed entire books of the Bible to memory. He often from memory recited various parts of Revelation, John, and several other

New Testament books. I believe one of the reasons my family came to America was through the fervent prayer of this small group that met weekly in Ben and Lauretta's home.

When Yah and the children arrived on March 9, 1995, we held their first Christmas party in this couple's home. Lauretta introduced our children to swimming in their pool as we made subsequent visits. One day we brought the children over for swimming and felt assured that they could now be on their own without much supervision. The adults pulled their chairs together on one side and became involved in a series of conversations that followed one after the other. Fortunately, Lauretta was the only person who understood what it meant to multi-task. Although she was deeply involved in the conversation, she was also constantly watching over the children. To our total surprise, we saw Lauretta quickly jump from her chair, run to the pool and dive right in to bring out Tonzia who was at the bottom! Lauretta later explained that she saw Tonzia struggling to come up and saw that she was drowning. Tonzia, to this date, has never forgotten this experience.

Unfortunately, the prayer group discontinued after I graduated and moved to Chicago in 1996 to begin a PhD program at Loyola University. The Pattersons eventually moved to Carpentaria, California, where Ben assumed a new position as chaplain for a small Christian college. Although the group members went in different directions, the relationship continued and later on transformed into a "ministry partnership" as we pursued our vision for developing a Christian college in Liberia. Lauretta and Ben continue to pray for our family and our ministry and they are among our faithful supporters. Lauretta still regularly sends me special notes to assure me of their prayer support and always encourages us in our missions and goals.

Between school, work and family, I didn't have much time left. But, in the back of my mind, however, I often thought about what it would take to establish a Christian college in Liberia. It didn't take me long to realize that I needed more experience and further training. I kept believing that God would guide our next steps to accomplish His vision.

Part III   Becoming Fully Equipped

Chapter 10   Rising to a New Challenge

As we approached the end of my studies at Western Theological Seminary, we began to pray for the Lord's direction for our next steps. The civil war in Liberia was still raging, making it impossible for us to safely return home. The best opportunity we saw was for me to find a school in the U.S. where I could continue my studies. By that point I was sick and tired of the classroom, but I could see no other way. I began to search for a new school and applied to various theological institutions to pursue another Master's or a Doctorate of Ministries.

Amos and Mary Miamen attending Graduation

The Van Wylens with Yah and Me

One day I decided to seek wisdom from Dr. Gordon Van Wylen. When Gordon asked me why I wanted to pursue my studies at a theological institution, I explained that I did not have the confidence to attend a secular university in America since I was a slow reader, and, moreover, my previous studies had related almost entirely to the Bible.

Gordon inspired me and challenged me; he said that I could make it! He explained to me that God wanted me to serve the world and not just the Church and that a large, secular university would give me a balanced education in order to be better equipped as a leader back in my country. The diverse faculty and broader range of courses would better prepare me for the responsibilities I would soon undertake. He promised to write all of my recommendations. He asked me to start my application process with the University of Michigan where he had served as a Chairman of the Engineering Department before becoming President of Hope College. From my discussion with Gordon, I was greatly inspired and determined not to narrowly focus on a theological education only but to now seek admission into a secular university. I started researching universities and began submitting applications.

One of the universities I looked at was Loyola. Loyola had a department for "Educational Leadership." I have a passion for leadership. I have a passion for education. My challenge was to eventually focus on the training of leaders rather than just personal theological education! This would be perfect for me. I would not only teach Christian truth but I could replicate myself by training future leaders of my country.

When I contacted the admission office of Loyola, I found out that they wanted me to take the Graduate Records Examination test (the GRE). I right away began studying for this difficult test. I worked on it as much as possible. In the meantime I ended up sending Loyola my thesis from Western Seminary. It was on "Transformational Leadership" and how these concepts can be applied in Liberia, indeed, in all of Africa to build the Church there. After I sent my Master's thesis, I received a response. Instead of having to do the GRE, on the basis of my thesis, I was accepted into the Comparative Education Department with an emphasis on educational leadership and administration.

Loyola is a Catholic school. I went to see my assigned advisor, Michael Perko, who was a Priest. I explained that I was an evangelical pastor and I had concerns about whether I would be expected to change or compromise my beliefs. Dr. Perko reviewed his files and began pulling out those of different students he had previously advised. The files he pulled were examples of different evangelical leaders who graduated from Loyola. He said to me, "If you are looking to learn a catechism, this is the wrong place. If you have a mindset for rigorous research, though, then this is the place for you." This helped put my mind at rest and made me more eager to begin my studies.

Now that I had been accepted there was one crucial challenge left. Again, the challenge was funding. First of all, I did not have a Green Card and so was not eligible to obtain any loans to fund my education. Secondly, I had a family of five who depended on me for their primary support. One day I drove to the admissions office in Chicago and the officer told me to deposit $35,000 or produce an affidavit of support to guarantee payment of $35,000! I returned to Holland that night thinking that the door to Loyola had closed on me since I had no means to produce such funds or anything even close to that amount.

That night our family came together and prayed. The next day I
went to Christ Memorial and shared the sad news with Pastor Dave
Kool and asked him if he could write a letter on my behalf. To my
total surprise he agreed to write the letter that very day. I explained
what the school was asking for and he made reference to that university
requirement. He wrote a few paragraphs and handed it over to me. I
drove again to Chicago and took the letter to the admissions office. The
administrative assistant accepted the letter and promised to process my
student F-1 immigration visa and mail it back to me in about two
weeks. The letter came in less than two weeks. I went to meet with
Dr. Van Wylen and shared the good news. During our conversation
he reached over on his shelf and brought out the church directory and
began to mark some of the names. In the end he showed me all the
names he had marked. He explained that those were his friends and
that I should write to all those friends to share the news about my
admission requirements and ask them for financial support.

He asked Pastor Dave Kool if the church would be able to accept
all gifts on my behalf and have the church forward them on to me.
Dave accepted the request and suggested that the letter be written on
the church's official letterhead to reinforce the appeal. In addition to
the tuition fees, we also included the amount for family support which
covered food, rent, etc.

In response to the first letter, the church informed us that more
than $12,000 had been raised for our support! I wrote a thank you
letter to all these new friends that gave and asked for prayer for God
to help us raise the balance needed. After writing the thank you letter,
additional gifts came in and we were set to go. In that same week Dave
Kool called and asked me to meet him at his office and go to lunch.
Dave said he had good news for me. I met with Dave that afternoon
and he informed me that a car dealer from the Church had offered us
a very reliable Mercury station wagon. After lunch we went to pick up
the car and bring it home. The final week of departure Dr. Gordon
called some friends together to serve as a committee to pray for our
family and about five couples promised to pray for our family diligently while we lived in Chicago.

We had mixed feelings about leaving, as you can imagine. God had worked many good and wonderful works through the people in Holland. In 1994, on the night I arrived, Dr. Gordon and Margaret Van Wylen became my first American friends in Holland. That same weekend they took me to Christ Memorial Church and it became my American home church. CMC's warm welcome to me personally and the leadership's confidence in my ministry calling had led to a succession of blessings and opportunities for myself and my family. From being their "missionary family in residence" to being sent out by them for further training, their generosity had blessed us beyond anything we could have imagined. Their love to us touched our family so deeply that our daughters both chose Hope College for their undergraduate studies.

Later, in 2002, we would receive from Christ Memorial Church our first and largest grant toward the development of Liberia International Christian College (LICC). I recount these stories to convey our sincere gratitude for God's faithfulness and the generosity of all the families of CMC. Their initial investment in our lives has brought educational blessings to my immediate family and now it is extending spiritually to the thousands of families in our nation of Liberia. We will never forget them.

The day came for us to leave Holland and move on to the next stage in our journey. We bid farewell to everyone and took off in our new station wagon for Chicago. We stopped in Wheaton, Illinois to visit with friends while we searched for our apartment. Our plans were proceeding smoothly, but there was yet another challenge ahead.

For three weeks all of our efforts to find an apartment resulted in our being turned down. The explanation was that we did not have a credit history. We saw a beautiful three-bedroom apartment in the city of Mount Prospect, but received the same explanation. The apartment manager asked if we could bring in someone to co-sign for us. We made a phone call to Gordon and Margaret and explained the situation. We left to visit a friend in Newark as we waited for the apartment to become available or for the Lord to provide us another place to live.

Gordon called us back to let us know that he had offered to co-sign for us, but the apartment refused to process it on the phone and wanted it to be done in person. The Van Wylens wanted us to know they were getting into the car to drive from Holland to Mount Prospect where they co-signed on our behalf. They drove over three hours each way. That is real commitment and Christian love.

When Gordon and Margaret drove from Holland to Mount Prospect to co-sign for the apartment, they drove through the community and found a Covenant Church sign. They let us know that they were familiar with the Covenant Church and knew it to be a good Bible-teaching Church. They suggested that we consider visiting it and, if we liked it, to make it our home church in Mount Prospect. It took us several weeks to locate that Church. Finally I found it one afternoon when I went to mail a letter at the post office. The problem was that in Mount Prospect there is an Elmhurst Road and an Elmhurst Street. The Church was located on Elmhurst Street. At the post office I saw the sign for the Church and followed it to the Church facility. I knocked at the door and the administrative assistant came out and introduced herself as Beth Peterson. Beth quickly took me to the senior pastor's office and introduced me to Dr. Herb Jacobson.

While we were in Newark, the day after Gordon and Margaret co-signed for us, the apartment management gave us a call to let us know that the apartment has been approved and that we could move into the apartment in about two weeks. When the appointed time came, we drove back to Mount Prospect and I went into the apartment office to receive the key. When I entered the office there were two ladies. The older woman took my file to make sure all of our information was correct. After a few minutes she looked at me and asked how many children we had. I replied that we had four, two boys and two girls. Then she said, "I am sorry. According to the rules, only five people are allowed in three bedroom apartments."

I explained that two of our boys will use one room and the two girls will have the second room while my wife and I get the third room. She re-stated that that was the local law and that she did not make the law of the city.

Suddenly, the second lady interrupted us and told the older lady that she was wrong and that our family was eligible for the apartment. Their conversation then erupted into a major argument. The older lady said she would not sign on our document, but the younger lady said she would sign it no matter what. The younger lady explained that there have been many cases perfectly similar to ours and those families were living in three bedroom apartments. In the end, the younger manager signed our paper and gave me the keys.

That same week we moved into the apartment. We did not have much, only the few things given to us from our friends in Holland. Only Yah's and my room had a bed. The children's rooms did not. When the previous tenants moved out, the apartment was cleaned very well. The carpet looked almost like brand new. The children put down their comforters on the carpet and slept on the floor. In less than a week another family moved out of an apartment just a few doors away and had a garage sale. We managed to purchase two beds for the girls. The two beds were almost new, and little-by-little the girls began to decorate their room. Over time, we found two beds at a garage sale for the boys' room. As we were able, we visited garage sales and eventually bought all our furniture at such sales.

Chapter 11   Academics and Part-Time Jobs

By 1996, my first semester of classes had started. I was registered as a full-time student at Loyola. There were about 17 students in our program, "Educational Leadership and Administration." I started with great zeal and excitement and was determined to not only get through the program, but to excel in my academic work. Once the classes were in full swing I applied for a job on campus and got a position as a library assistant on the Loyola Wilmette campus. My responsibilities included shelving books, making copies, ordering inter-library loan books for students, and assisting students and faculty in finding reference materials (or articles online). The school was paying me $7.50 per hour for about 20 hours per week. I felt very fortunate. This was a good supplement to the factory job that Yah was able to obtain.

One evening a professor, Dr. Walter Krolikowski, came to the library looking for an article. He made several searches but could not locate what he needed. I saw that he was getting frustrated and asked if I could help. I found the materials outside of Loyola, promised to request the materials from the other library, and explained to him that I would contact him once the materials came in. In a couple of days the materials arrived and I took them to his office. He was a professor of philosophy and value theory. When I arrived at his office, he asked me to sit down and we entered into a brief conversation. He explained that he was a Catholic priest and had been teaching at the University for almost 40 years. He told me a bit about his family background. His parents had come from Poland, he had been born in Chicago, and he had attended Catholic schools which had influenced his life and his eventual calling to the priesthood.

When the first semester ended, there were vacancies in my department for graduate teaching and research assistants. I applied for the research assistant position. There were several other applications that came in as well. The requirements were that you must be a full-time student, have a high GPA, and have a previous knowledge of computers. Indeed, I had met all of these criteria. In addition, I asked Dr. Krolikowski for a recommendation and he gladly wrote one for me. I asked the department chairman, Dr. Erwin Epstein, as well, and he also agreed to write a recommendation. My job in the library had helped me not only to know all the professors, and most of the students, but also to find great friends and advocates.

In the end, I was awarded a research assistant position in the Department of Educational Leadership and Administration. I was assigned to two professors, Dr. Krolikowski and Dr. Epstein! The position offered me a 100% scholarship and a $200 monthly stipend. I wrote to my Christ Memorial friends in Holland and shared the unbelievable news that I would not need support anymore for tuition beginning the second semester. However, I still needed their support to cover food and monthly rent which was $960 for the apartment in Mount Prospect. I scheduled my work with the assigned professors. The workload was very reasonable and I only worked when there was work available for me to do. I decided to take advantage of my spare time and the many opportunities before me.

As I look back on my time there, Loyola affected me in several ways. One of the most prominent ways was that I developed my analytical broad-based critical thinking skills. In theology school we learned about the truth of Scripture. At Loyola we were taught to use other disciplines to solve problems that weren't as easy as providing a biblical reference from the Bible. I discovered the importance of good reasoning and research in all areas of life. I now had fine tuned my world view without compromising the truths of Scripture. We studied philosophy, sociology, and history, and I always looked at these disciplines in the light of Scripture. All "truth" is God's truth. This would help me later when designing a curriculum for a Christian college. I would work to make the college interdenominational that not only prepared theological thinkers but would be an institution to train the future leaders of Liberia in many career areas of life.

*   *   *   *   *   *   *   *   *   *   *   *

I was very busy at Loyola but that did not keep me from keeping up with the ongoing conflict in my home country. The Liberian civil war had a devastating effect on everyone. From first indications of instability and unrest until a lasting peace was achieved spanned nearly 14 years, the first civil war from 1989-1996 and the second from

1999-2003. There was a severe decrease in the gross domestic product accompanied by a decline in economic and social development. What little money existed was mostly spent on the military. This had a grave negative impact on health care, social infrastructure, and education. Maintenance of child welfare clinics and immunization programs was compromised. Life expectancy decreased and there was a higher infant mortality rate, also. During the war years most of the medical resources were focused on the war effort and to maintain health services for the combatants.

Malnutrition became common. It had always plagued Africa even without war, but now it became worse. Once someone was ill or was injured there most likely would not be any doctor or even a health-care worker in the vicinity. The young and the old suffered the most. Many many children and older people died. Even traveling to seek help became more difficult. Roads and bridges fell into disrepair and bus services stopped operation. In many areas it was just unsafe to travel. Looking back, I knew that the Lord had prepared my family to leave the country in His time! My heart, though, still ached for my people and my land.

The war also devastated the school system. For the young in the countryside, the chance to pursue an education had become non-existent. In many cases the schools never reopened. Those children in urban areas remained in school, but were under constant fear and faced frequent disruption of their classes. Most of the qualified teachers in secondary schools and the professors at the universities were killed or fled from the country. Initially, some of the neighboring countries offered limited educational opportunities to refugee children. However, education for refugees in the Ivory Coast (Cote d'Ivoire) and Guinea was problematic because the language of those countries is French, not the English spoken in Liberia.

During the war thousands of Liberians sought refuge in various countries, primarily Ivory Coast, Guinea and Sierra Leone. The continuing influx of displaced persons and refugees across their borders during this time period led to regional problems in these host countries, such as shortages of food and ethnic tensions. Also, there were natural environmental problems like droughts that made the situation worse. In some of these neighboring countries ethnic ties were strong and refugees were treated kindly. In others, ethnic ties were weaker and local soldiers constantly harassed refugees. Most of the displaced people lived in overcrowded tents in refugee camps with very few resources. In the most remote areas villagers could not afford to escape to neighboring countries for safety; instead they fled into the bush.

In 1999, however, while I was at Loyola, the civil war in Liberia began to slow down. Fifteen thousand United Nations peacekeeping soldiers entered the country and in a short time they began a massive disarmament program. The promise of free and fair elections convinced both the rebels and ordinary Liberians to lay down their arms. With this message, the rebels saw the opportunity to transform their groups into political parties rather than fighting forces. As a result, there were 48 political parties registered to take part in a free and fair election. This was the first of its kind in Liberian history. The political parties began recruiting members in Liberia and also in America. Thousands of people joined political parties.

I love my country and I love its people because it is my home and the home of my family. As a Christian I also love them with the love of Christ. After the bloody civil war, enduring peace was a welcome and good thing. However, as I reflected on the civil war, two questions dominated my mind. The first question was, "What led us into war in the first place?" The second question was, "What are the most effective ways to address and solve such problems so that our future will no longer be threatened?" I was specifically determined to find some sort of biblical resolution that could apply to our country's conflicts and possibly eliminate civil war altogether in our nation at any time in the future.

As I reflected on these questions in various forms and became more analytical about it, I sensed the Lord beginning to enlighten my mind and directing me to recall the conference I attended in a small village with about fifty Liberian Christian leaders back in 1994. This was during my time in Gambia when I had gone back to visit my country. During the conference I received what I clearly perceived as "God's commission" through the request of the leaders to develop a college for leadership training.

I had just finished preaching and challenging these leaders to remain faithful to the Lord in the midst of their adversity. The leaders there faced great adversity. I illustrated my point with the Apostle Paul's encounter in the book of Acts (Acts 26), where the Islanders expected him to die after been bitten by a deadly viper. When Paul sought the Lord the viper dropped dead as the mighty power of God delivered His servant.

The worst part of it was the seeming hopelessness of the situation – at least from human eyes. At that time the civil war was ongoing with no end in sight. We didn't know if when the end came, whether it would be even worse than the civil war itself. What good did it do for them to have faith? What good did it do for them to believe? There was no medicine available and very limited medical care. The older people, the foundation of the church, were particularly at risk. They were dying regularly from poor health conditions. We mourned for them even though we knew they went to a better place in heaven than our war-torn country. We also, though, had to be concerned about those who remained. We all worried about the ones that would "step into their shoes" as leaders of the Church.

When I had shared from my heart before those fifty Liberian Christian leaders, I had seen in their faces the crushing weight of adversity. What could I say to these people? What theology could I offer? What message could comfort them? What words could I give them to address the real gravity of their situation? How does faith work in a time like this? I thought about my training in the Bible. I thought of the many men who faced adversity in biblical times – the heroes of our faith. Of those many heroes of the faith, Paul came to my mind. So I told them the story of Paul when he was shipwrecked on Crete. As I told the story, I could see a change in the countenances of some of the leaders. I could see understanding shine in some of their faces. I could see the glimmer of hope begin to encourage them. I asked them to share what they had received with their neighbors and many did just that. This experience would years later help me realize the importance of building first a solid foundation of God's Word into the lives of future leaders. Not just for church leaders, but Liberia's new business leaders and political leaders needed to know the ethics of the kingdom of God.

No one person or even small groups of people could personally minister to all of the needs of all of the Liberians. We could, however, equip the leaders to train leaders so that everyone could be reached with the wisdom that comes from God alone. We could multiply our efforts to nourish the faith of thousands.

So it was during my time at Loyola that I began taking the first practical steps towards the vision for a Liberian Christian University. It started in a very small way. As refugees started coming to the area, Yah and I would meet with them for fellowship. At first this was quite informal. However, we began to do this more regularly as a group. It was through these groups that I started sharing my vision with my fellow Liberians.

This was a time of change that represented an opportunity to impact our country. For example, for the first time in the history of Liberia, a woman was elected President. It showed the power of democracy at work. In a state of civil war it would have been impossible for us to do what we would end up doing in Liberia. So the arrival of democracy brought real benefits because it allowed Liberians to take responsibility for their own future to build a better Liberia – a Liberia established in biblical faith.

Before the civil war ended there were very few opportunities for women to obtain leadership positions in any area of life. Education opportunities were minimal. Yet, at the end of the civil war, Liberians voted for a woman, a mother, educated in America, that was respected both within and outside of Liberia. She had attended Harvard University. Her example has inspired women to get involved in government, in business, and in all of society. Because of her example more young girls are making the decision to get an education. As informed and well-trained and educated women, they want to be an important part of this rebuilding process in Liberia.

*   *   *   *   *   *   *   *   *   *   *

I sometimes feel like I have spent my whole life going to school! But that doesn't mean I haven't worked. Indeed, it also seems like I was constantly looking for ways to support my family while I studied. I appreciated the help and generosity provided by others and I was fortunate that Yah was so resourceful, but I knew it was important for me to work to help provide for myself and my family as well.

While studying at Loyola, one day I stopped by a delivery company and asked if I could do some extra work for them whenever my schedule permitted. The manager accepted my offer, but on the condition that I use my own car for the deliveries. We made an arrangement for me to call in for jobs whenever I had time available. The company agreed to pay me 60% of the price they charged customers for delivering packages plus an outside-city-limit mileage charge of twenty-five cents per mile. I took the job and was doing quite well bringing in some extra income to help the family, and also so that I could purchase books and supplies.

The business started well, but I was putting a lot of miles on the family car very rapidly which led to more frequent car repairs. By this time we had opened both savings and checking accounts with Bank One in Mount Prospect. The bank was only a few blocks from our apartment, and so I made frequent visits there. Some of the people were very friendly and would chat with me when I went into the bank.

One day I indicated to one of the employees that I was thinking about trying to get a loan to purchase a more reliable van for my delivery business. I explained to him up front that I was a foreign student and not a citizen and that I didn't even have a Green Card. After my explanation, he turned to me and said that those issues had nothing to do with me getting a loan. This surprised me a bit. He continued sharing that in order to get a loan they needed to know if I had a job. I told him about my research assistant job at Loyola and the delivery job.

Upon hearing the Loyola name, he asked again, "Did you say you are a PhD student?"

I replied, "Yes."

Then he said, "Do you have a document to prove that you are a full-time PhD student? And, do you have one of your last two most current pay slips?" I replied in the affirmative. Then he said, "If you can bring those to me by tomorrow, I will be in a better position to answer your question about the loan."

The next day I returned with all the documents he had requested. He asked me to give him a couple of days to process things for me. The following day, when I returned from school, my children told me the man from the bank had called and left a message asking me to stop by his office.

The next morning I stopped to see him again and he said the documents were great, but I fell short because I had no past credit history. He suggested that I go to a Chevrolet dealer nearby, obtain a car with a car loan from them, and then bring the loan document to him. This was somewhat curious. My Bank One friend then explained the strategy to me. If I started by applying for a bank loan without any credit history I could be denied. If, however, I started with a car dealer, I would likely be able to purchase a car with one of their loans, but with a very high interest rate. We would then apply for the bank loan based on my having successfully obtained a car loan. The strategy worked and I got a Chevy-G20 with 32,000 miles for $10,000 at 21% interest rate. I then returned to the bank with all the documents, and the following day my banker got me a new loan for a little over $10,000 from the bank at 8.25% interest rate. This took two days to process and I was in business with a nearly new van at a competitive interest rate and, at the same time, I was also establishing a credit history in America!

The delivery business began to grow and I was soon delivering luggage from O'Hare and Midway Airports from delayed or cancelled airline flights. The Lord blessed my efforts and I was able to pay the loan off within two years! These work related experiences have helped me see the need to establish "micro-loans" to struggling Liberians that would provide initial start-up money to enable them to become self-sufficient. God would use everything I went through to help me prepare these future leaders.

In the meantime our relationship with Northwest Covenant Church was growing too. Like my home church in Holland, the Covenant Church congregation consisted of all white people, but this time almost all of them were of Swedish descent (rather than reformed Dutch). But, they showed us the same Christian love in every manner. Dr. Jacobsen, the senior pastor, was a retired professor of Theology from Wheaton Graduate School. He became our family friend and also a father to all our children. Rev. Paul Thompson, his Associate Pastor (and youth Pastor), was a very friendly man and developed close relationships with all of my children as well. I began teaching a Sunday school class called "International Bible Study" and many adults participated. Occasionally, Pastor Jacobsen would ask me to preach in the church. The church leadership asked me to serve on the church mission board, and I gladly accepted.

One day a notice was placed in the bulletin that the custodian was moving and the church needed a replacement. Our family applied for the job and we began to clean the church once a week on Saturday evenings. Now, we had three part time jobs which equaled one full-time job. By giving us this work, the Lord blessed us and allowed us to not only care for our family but to teach our children the importance of their contribution to reaching our future ministry goals. It would be excellent preparation for the many jobs they would eventually have.

Lily was eighteen and Tonzia was fourteen, so they could do nearly any task that an adult could do. Deizie was twelve and Ben was nine and they loved to help. With the four of them at work, the jobs went very quickly. Lily had already held down part-time jobs at Dominic's (a grocery store) and at Jungle gyms for children.

Chapter 12   The Seed Grows: Advice
of Godly Men

As I started working out my vision for a Liberian Christian college, I realized I would need assistance and sound advice from many different types of professionals and godly leaders. The vision seemed clear enough but how was I to fulfill it? I turned to two men who were quite familiar with ministries in Africa – one in America and the other in the United Kingdom.

The first man, Mr. Newman, was an American missionary who had served in Kenya, East Africa, for over twenty years. He knew the African cultural setting.

I really did believe that God was calling me, but why did I sense some reluctance? Well, it was partly because I was undertaking a project for which I had absolutely no previous experience. After all, what kind of a foreign graduate student walks around saying, "I'm going to go start a college!" I could only go so far on my enthusiasm.

Also, where would the money come from? While this wouldn't be the typical missionary effort spearheaded by Westerners, we would definitely need help from the West in order to make it happen. Would the western church support an indigenous work led by this African Liberian? The vision seemed clear to me, but how would I convince other Christian leaders, pastors and educators that they could trust me with the finances?

These questions and concerns led me to consult with this first godly man. I had many reasons for going to him for advice, but mainly I knew that he had raised his own personal support for many years, so he knew what I was facing. I looked forward to his guidance.

I was visiting Phil and Amber Synder in Zeeland, Michigan when I first met Mr. Newman and his family. The family had come home on a furlough for much need rest and to raise their on-going support needs. I shared my vision about starting a Christian College in Liberia and expressed my money concerns. He exhorted me to move ahead with the vision and "let God do the rest." He explained to me that in the past, American Churches that tended to work mostly through their own denominations were often bound by conservative boards and narrowly focused on their own works. He said that this was changing radically. He pointed out that while in the past only Westerners were regarded as missionaries worthy of denominational or American support, today there was a growing desire to help indigenous leaders take control of their own churches and missions endeavors. It seemed like I was developing this vision at the right time in world missionary history. He said that many Americans would be willing to partner with us to rebuild Liberia and advance the good news of Christ. His unabashed confidence in what God would do and his keen observation that the vision was timely encouraged me tremendously.

Typically, only large denominations or established mission groups would take on the task we felt compelled by God to tackle. WEC (Worldwide Evangelization for Christ International) was the organization I had worked with in Gambia. They had been working with missionaries all over the world. Our organization was springing forth from poor Liberian refugees! This was counter revolutionary. New mission works were just not started from such humble beginnings, or at least I thought so!

The second godly man I consulted was Mr. Bill Chapman, a WEC International Education Consultant for Africa. He was the local expert for WEC. I was hoping Bill could give me some advice on this project. Later that year, I gratefully received a detailed response from Bill regarding my general education questions. He too strongly exhorted me to lead the effort and to move forward.

Bill, however, clearly advised against starting a denominational Bible College. Instead, he encouraged me to follow the example of the Ghana Christian Service College in West Africa. I had personally visited this college in 1994 and had spoken with many of their professors and administrative leaders. The college first started as a denominational institution, but it made no impact until it changed its status to nondenominational. My eventual commissioning at the Liberia leaders' conference in addition to these words of wisdom from these two men, made it clear to me that I was to move forward with the plan to open a Christian college in Liberia. I had come to believe that the problem in our country was a lack of "trained and faithful men." We needed men with training that were willing to train other faithful men, who would do the same for coming generations. This followed the Biblical principle taught by Paul in II Timothy 2:2: *"And the things you have heard me say in the presence of many witnesses entrust to reliable men who will also be qualified to teach others."*

Sometimes in the past, Liberia had had leaders that were self-centered and preoccupied with only short-term goals and self-serving. The end result often was the self-destruction of our entire nation.

Bill also cautioned me to be sure that I had received a calling from God before launching the vision. Human strength would carry me only so far – I could easily fail. He continually emphasized that it should be "non-denominational." He knew that a denominational school would not win the hearts and minds of many gifted people who had a commitment to help the "whole" body of Christ. He said that we should pray that God would bring us the right people with the right interest and skills to do the work, regardless of denomination. We needed to stress our purpose, which was the building of the Kingdom of God in Africa through the training of Christian leaders.

With God anything is possible, and the building of a college would require great wisdom and much practical help. The vision eventually was confirmed, but it wouldn't just spring out of the ground. Even in Liberia it cost quite a large sum of money to build a college.

We had been working together and praying for each other. Now was time for action. Where should we start? Where should we begin? I made an appointment with Dr. Gordon Van Wylen (President of Hope College) to talk about a funding strategy. To start with, we did a direct mailing. Since I was a member of the Reformed Church I started with my local church. We wrote our first grant proposal to Christ Memorial Church in Holland. God and the church were faithful and we received an initial $28,000! We did not have a 501(c)(3) status at the time, so we asked the church to keep the money for a future donation to the ministry. Dr. Van Wylen also wrote a few letters to some of his best friends and we received overwhelming responses from all of them.

I should explain something about my mission background. I was taught in my mission background to never ask anyone for money. If you had a need, you were told to ask God first. This was a way of training us to rely wholly on God to provide. If someone heard our story and came and said, "What do you need?" then we could tell them what the need was. Now I was being told to tell everyone what our financial needs were. This created in me a great emotional and spiritual conflict. I felt strongly that we should just ask God for help. We should let God provide as needed.

Gordon had a different strategy and view. He told me, "With Americans, you have to ask for what you need." He indicated that Americans will go and ask a businessperson for a $50,000 loan. That concept was foreign to me. That much money would be a fortune – so we started with smaller requests. Gordon set up appointments with groups and I did speaking engagements. We started sharing our story and vision at small luncheons. I spoke to people about our dream for Liberia and asked them to help us make it possible.

On a side note, early on people would ask me what the total project cost would be. I had never started a university or anything like this before, so I didn't know. I could give an estimate, but I had no idea what even the building costs would be.

Part IV From Vision To Reality

Chapter 13   God Works Through a Conference

The Liberian refugee community from rural Liberia originally formed separate fellowship groups in different areas of America. For example, there was one fellowship group in Chicago and another in Florida. We were all now finally coming together from across the nation. Everyone wanted to know what he or she could do to rebuild our nation. The initial group that was started by students had dissolved and then reorganized to include whole Liberian families that could pool their resources and work on a more comprehensive strategy to help our country.

On June 13, 2000, twenty-two participants met at the University of Indianapolis for the first time under the name of Liberian Refugee Fellowship. Shadrach Gonqueh, a Liberian student at the university, coordinated this meeting. We elected leaders to begin developing the first steps of our vision. They created enthusiasm for fellowship and spiritual growth among our local membership.

We next planned to host an all Liberian Christian conference June 22-24, 2001 at The Northwest Covenant Church in Mount Prospect, Illinois. Pastor Jacobsen, the senior pastor, accepted our invitation to be our keynote speaker. Sixty-seven adults attended from many cities and states which was the largest number of Liberians we had ever gathered. We enhanced our relationships and all took ownership of the vision. Participants had a wonderful uplifting time, enjoying unique opportunities to create or enhance relationships with each other. I challenged the group to make some tangible commitments, and they did. But, in order for a vision to really take shape and begin to move people forward, it had to be heard and owned by many more people within and outside of the group.

Some of the students were interested in politics believing this was the pathway to peace. But they wondered: "What role would our faith play?" There were many challenges. Most of the refugees either had no skills or were struggling students that could barely pay for their own college costs. Other refugees worked two or three jobs to make ends meet. I understood their situation because I had endured through similar hard times. We knew the importance of everyone being involved in the vision and so we encouraged even modest giving.

We asked that the members give at least $10 monthly and obviously more if they had the means! Some gave part of their tithe and others at great sacrifice gave $1,000 or more a year.

These refugees that supported the ministry had to move often as their work and financial situation changed, and so their mailing addresses changed frequently. They kept the vision because of their zeal to make a difference in our homeland Liberia.

On the final day of the Liberian conference the participants made three commitments: (1) to purchase suitable land for a Bible College in Ganta, (2) to construct an Inland Church headquarters building in Monrovia, and (3) to construct a local church in Saclepea, a small city thirty-five miles south of Ganta.

*　　*　　*　　*　　*　　*　　*　　*　　*　　*　　*　　*

They all faced difficult cultural challenges. In Africa the wife cleans the home, cooks the food, and washes the dishes. However, when they came to America, both husband and wife have to secure jobs just to get by; often at least one of them will work two jobs. The husband, however, still expects his wife to do all of the housework. This creates a lot of stress in the couple's relationship. Also, for the first time with both parents working, the children were often left home alone. Unfortunately, unsupervised children might join gangs or the girls could get pregnant at an early age.

I was a minister to this community and a pastor for these people wherever they lived. Yah and I counseled with husbands and wives –sometimes ending up as a day and night job. We would get calls at all hours and hear confessions as, "My husband is beating me" or "My wife is leaving me." When I was able, I often helped them with their practical problems. For example, one couple's car would not run because of transmission problems and could not get to work and thus could not provide for their family. They may be without cash or credit to even make the repair and we would help them. I even one time bought a transmission for someone on my own credit card. The recipient paid me back one small payment at a time, although I had to cover the interest myself. We had been graciously provided for by the Lord and his people, so we gave back in such ways when we were able.

For students we were close to we might provide meals for them and for pregnant women Yah would cook soup. It was a special African pepper soup with hot spices and a little beef or chicken. In Liberia, to make soup, you cook with the bones. Other times, we would take care of their children. Yah and I often babysat for their children. We have now seen some of the fruit of their struggles and challenges. Some have now graduated and started businesses and professional careers and are now able to give back to the ministry. Several of our students, Dr. Shadrach Gonqueh (a dentist) and three registered nurses, Ellen Karnweah-Tuah, Dorene Gono and Lily Buor, became extremely passionate about our plan to establish a health center on the college campus. They decided that providing health services to all of our students and staff was a unique opportunity for Liberia and essential for our ministry and made generous financial contributions toward the project cost.

Prior to the establishing of LICC, we introduced two ministry initiatives. *The Hope Farm* was birthed through the compassion of Lee and Narko Wuanti who suffered first hand from hunger while growing up in their village. Hunger has been for decades a chronic problem for Liberian farmers who have been in dire need of assistance with new methods and resources. *Hope Farm* was established to assist local farmers who were returning to their villages to become self-reliant and sustain their families. *The One Hour for Christ Scholarship* was developed because of Lydia and Foster's passion for sponsorship of young women whose parents are either dead or unable to provide them the right opportunities. Lydia explained that the Lord laid the scholarship assistance on her heart because of the struggle she had in finishing school; it was only through her older sister's help that she graduated. Through *One Hour for Christ Scholarship* young girls and women are provided with resources needed to aid in their education. The scholarship covers the student's books, transportation, and tuition. These young women are encouraged to return to serve Liberia through their different fields and in turn support *One Hour for Christ* for the next generation.

These are just some examples of young students who were now maturing into our future leaders. The time had come when we would soon be relying on them to take the next step of actually purchasing the ground and building the first phase of the school.

Chapter 14 Our Plans Are Changed… Again

In 2001, we planned to return to Liberia immediately after my graduation from Loyola University. So, we began all the needed preparations for the transition. First, we continued to raise funds for the development of Liberia International Christian College. The Lord blessed us with the ability to raise the $50,000 which we felt was enough to start the college.

Loyola Graduation

Secondly, we wrote a letter to Dr. James Bultman, President of Hope College, letting him know of our plans for returning to Liberia. We also appealed for full scholarship assistance for our two daughters, Lily and Tonzia, who were studying at Hope. Our request was granted, and the school gave generous scholarships to the girls which allowed them both to graduate from Hope. Finally, we asked a couple from Northwest Covenant Church in Mount Prospect to serve as legal guardians for our two boys. As far as our plans were concerned, we had everything under control and only had to await my graduation from Loyola. Immediately following my graduation, we gave up our apartment and went to live with a missionary friend. We did some last minute shopping and purchased what we would need when we arrived in Liberia. Then we went ahead and shipped several barrels of clothing, bedding, computers, etc. for our anticipated arrival.

Before the actual departure, we decided to make a final trip to Florida to visit some friends. But a single phone call that came at that time changed the whole course of our lives. We received a call from a church leader in Liberia. They said we should postpone the return and await further instructions. The church leader explained that one of the major rebel groups had attacked the capital city of Monrovia and serious fighting had begun. The government of Charles Taylor had declared a state of emergency. The declaration allowed security personnel to arrest anyone found to be suspicious or who was suspected to be a sympathizer with the rebels. All international news coming from the area confirmed the church leader's report. Our departure plans fell apart. Now what?

We had given away our apartment, shipped all our belongings to Liberia, and the children were settled in their various locations, but the door had again been shut for our return. A couple of days after this call, another call came in, but this call was to provide some relief from our current predicament. A friend called from Carmel, Indiana to find out about our exact date of departure because he wanted to know if we could take something back to Liberia for his wife. We explained the story and the current situation in Liberia. In the conversation, my friend offered us a room in which to stay while we waited for the door to Liberia to reopen.

So it was in 2002 that Yah and I arrived in Carmel, Indiana, without any of our children and with very few belongings at the invitation of our dear friend Joseph Gbor. Our friend was renting a small cottage in the city of Carmel, a northern suburb of Indianapolis. When we arrived my friend suggested that we meet with the property owner, Ruth Schwartz, and confirm her approval for us to stay in the cottage with him. He drove us to Grace Community Church where we met Ruth. Joseph carefully explained who we were and some details of our situation. He also explained to Ruth that he would like to offer us one of the rooms in the cottage until the situation in Liberia improved enough to allow for our return.

In response, Ruth said, "Go ahead."

This indicated to Yah and me that she approved our friend's request! We returned to the little cottage and settled in. Day-after-day turned into month-after-month of waiting to get a call from Liberia about our return. But, after three months, it became clear to us that our desire for quick departure was not going to be possible. By that time we had come to accept that God had temporarily closed the door for our immediate return to Liberia. Next, we decided that we would pray and wait on the Lord for some clarification or for a new direction in our lives. During this time we were also made aware of the problems we would cause our children if we left the United States since their visa status was dependent on my visa and my being in the US. It was not too long after we had resigned ourselves to the fact that we would be in America for awhile that the Lord began to unfold what He wanted us to do, how He would work to bring about His plans, and how we were right where He needed us to be to fulfill our part of His plans.

The Schwartz's own home property is huge. They use a tractor to cut the lawn. As a way to release my frustration I asked Ruth if I could use the tractor to cut the grass around both houses, their main house and the cottage. She agreed, and every other week I would get on the tractor and cut the grass. After cutting, Ruth would come by the cottage and write me a check. At first, I resisted the check. But, she would not let me work for her without any payment. One day in our conversation, I referred to Ruth as our "landlord." Immediately, I saw her facial expression change and she said to me, "Please never call me your landlord; I am not your landlord. You are my brother, and I am your sister in Christ Jesus."

Uncontrollable tears filled my eyes, and I looked around to determine who was uttering these words. There wasn't anybody there except Ruth!

From then on the lesson was very clear. The faithful Lord had brought me and Yah to unite us with our sister in Christ who, along with her husband, would soon become a "vision partners" with us in His service. (Today, Ruth and her husband Russ are our executive volunteers. Ruth is on our ULICAF board and serves as our financial manager.)

Ruth's husband, Russ, appeared to be a very quiet man – gifted, intelligent and very creative. He left very early for work and returned around 5:00 p.m. I began to wonder why Russ was so quiet and why I never saw him with friends or saw any of his friends come by. However, one day, I saw him behind their house which faced our cottage. I saw him measuring the outside floor. After observing this measurement process over a couple of incidences, I saw some outdoor tile workers came to the house and lay beautiful tiles both in the front and back.

I was so impressed with the design that I chatted with him about it, and asked him about his background in such matters. He told me that he had been doing architectural things since he was 12 years old. In fact, for his fifteenth birthday he received a professional drawing board and drafting set. By the time he was a sophomore in high school he was a finalist in an architectural design competition sponsored by the Toledo branch of the American Institute of Architects. He had hoped to major in Architecture at the University of Cincinnati, but by his senior year of high school, he realized that all the fields and orchards around his house were becoming housing subdivisions. Feeling that as an architect he would be contributing to the "problem," he decided to go to DePauw University and enroll in Liberal Arts.

He did take some architectural design courses in school, but majored in psychology. As a result, he now works with computers at a major pharmaceutical corporation in Indianapolis, Eli Lilly & Co.

His interest in architecture was reawakened when he purchased Christopher Alexander's book *A Pattern Language* which gave him a deep understanding about what could be right and wrong about spaces. The new front porch and back patio were results of his study of that book.

I felt the Lord's leading, and I asked Russ if he would be willing to design a college building for me to be built in Liberia. Thus began many Wednesday evenings of getting to know each other, sharing the vision, tossing ideas around concerning the design of the college and its buildings, and eventually putting plans on paper for a campus and its buildings. Russ has spent literally hundreds of hours researching, designing and redesigning the structures. What started as a page of notes eventually mushroomed into a 6-inch stack of drawings and documentation – and is still growing.

Joseph, our friend, was also a member of Grace Community Church, so we became part of Grace Community Church. We loved everything about Grace: the vibrant preaching from the Bible, the people, and the small groups we were part of. We had found a new church home.

After ten months of waiting on the Lord, He spoke to me through my devotional time with Him that I should begin a job search that He would lead us to Liberia when the time was right. I was offered employment at the Indianapolis Public Schools where I was assigned as a teaching assistant at John Marshall Middle School. My specific assignment was to teach children with learning disabilities. In my graduate studies I studied special education, but never expected to have a practical role in the classroom. And, little did I know that the Lord brought me to these children to teach me some unique lessons in life.

First, the Lord humbled me by observing. About 90% of the children in my class were foster children. That meant their biological parents had given them up, usually through their behavior or life decisions because they were unable to care for their needs. They had turned them over to the state and to social workers in the foster home program. Many of the rest of the children lived with their grandmothers. Several of the students explained that their biological parents were alcoholics or in prison for using or selling drugs.

For the previous ten months I had been praying, but I had also been complaining quite loudly to God about the door being close to our return to Liberia. The children with learning disabilities only knew what was put before them. I struggled to help them write their own names. It took patience to deal with them. One day my head teacher walked in on me while I was teaching one of the boys how to write his full name. She stopped me and said, "You think you want to prepare him for a university, do you?" I replied, "Yes, I would love to teach him to be able to enter a university if I can." The head teacher told me, "No. All the children need are basic things to be able to live their life one day at a time." She also explained that many of the children would not even live to be twenty or twenty-five years old due to violence and drugs in the community.

One of the boys, Kyle repeatedly said to me, "Mr. Buor, I want to be like you, dress like you and walk like you." Another boy, Jimmie, suffered from muscular dystrophy and was in a wheelchair. One day, I took Jimmie out to play with the other boys. He saw a boy running with speed and he pointed at the boy and told me, "Mr. Buor that is how I used to run when I was small, but now I cannot because I am always sitting in my chair." I began to weep over this sixth-grade boy who was completely paralyzed from the waist down. I served at John Marshall Middle School for two years. Although I did not receive a degree for the work I did there, I learned anew one of life's most valuable lessons. I learned that I needed to appreciate everything I have been blessed with in this life.

Meanwhile, I did not waver in my commitment to the college. From a practical standpoint, over time, the Lord brought two important "vision partners" into my life. In July 2003, I had the opportunity to be a part of the Willow Creek Association Leadership Summit at Grace Community Church. Every year, the summit brings together thousands of leaders from across the nations and from various regional levels. It was at this summit that I first met my good friend John Lieberman. John has Jewish roots, but he is a mature believer in Christ, and led a Friday morning men's Bible study at Grace Community Church. John and I became friends instantaneously as though we had spent time together thousands of times and known each other for decades. We had many things in common, but the one thing that stands out clearly is that we both talk endlessly. However, John surpassed me with his many questions about my life, family, ministry, Liberia and theological issues. John became a key person in encouraging and challenging me to be courageous and to remain steadfastly open to what God has called me to do in Liberia.

John has served on the Board of LICC (Liberia International Christian College), and currently he is our Newsletter Editor and a great vision partner in the ministry. John and I are joined with a few other men that meet every Friday morning and study the Bible and pray at Grace Community Church.

As people like John started joining with us, we began to refine the purpose of ULICAF (United Liberia Inland Church Association and

Friends). As you will remember, ULICAF was born out of compassion in late 2000 as an informal organization of Liberian and American Christians for the purposes of providing faith-based fellowship and encouragement to refugees resettled in the United States, and providing spiritual and humanitarian support for the nation of Liberia.

Our organization continued to develop. Since 1999, we have hosted the Liberian conference in various states and cities in America. By 2003 we began to realize that for ULICAF to accomplish any of the goals we might have for it, we needed to actually put those goals into words. About that time, I began to seek ways to better understand the workings of a not-for-profit organization in the United States. As I read and talked with people I learned about mission statements and vision, strategic plans and risk management plans. The result of my inquiries was the opportunity to work with several not-for-profit Christian organizations through a Truth@work Roundtable to learn more.

Truth@work (www.truthatwork.org) is the result of a vision that was birthed in the heart of Ray Hilbert beginning in 1997. That vision was a culmination of personal, professional, and spiritual experiences that he experienced over the course of a decade after graduating from college with a business degree in 1988. Its mission is to equip today's Christian leaders to impact the market place.

In 2006, I joined a Truth@work Roundtable Group which is comprised of 10 to 12 executive directors and meets once a month to share in a synergistic exercise designed to increase our abilities and skills in building and leading our organizations. For two years we have been meeting to discuss issues and challenges in light of biblical principles and to pray for and with one another. Each participant is required to complete a personal and business assessment which is used to establish goals and commitment in all key areas of life - business, personal, family, spiritual. The members of the group hold each other accountable to accomplish these goals. From this group I also benefited from the insight and counsel of other executives. I specifically, learned about fund-raising strategies, how to develop a one-page businesses plan, and how to recruit new board members and volunteers effectively.

The vision for our organization (ULICAF) was for it to be a model and to be strategically positioned as *a Christ-centered vehicle for delivering humanitarian and spiritual support to all the churches and people groups in all of Liberia and neighboring countries without regard to ethnicity or national origin, while creating opportunities for self sufficiency* (Col. 3:12-14; Neh. 6.9).

The vision was followed by this mission statement: "To mobilize Liberians in the United States and American Christians and related organizations as a Christ-centered vehicle to provide humanitarian and spiritual support for indigenous churches and people in Liberia and for Liberians living in the United States, as they may need." Though ULICAF's primary affiliation in Liberia is the United Liberia Inland Church, its concerns embrace all churches and people.

ULICAF's mission was built upon the core values of the Bible.

- First and foremost, we desire to know Jesus Christ and make Him known.

- Second, we want to reveal God in relevant and innovative ways to our generation and generations to come.

- Finally, we wish to model Christ to all people without any regard to ethnicity, socio-economic standing, religion, and national background.

- ULICAF is dedicated to making a difference in the lives of Liberian immigrants in the United States, other nationalities and the nation of Liberia. We wanted to host annual Christian conferences, provide leadership training and develop cultural capacity and leadership skills that prepare ULICAF's members to become productive citizens in America.

- **Spiritual:** We knew our primary focus would be to spread the gospel of our Lord Jesus Christ through evangelism, church planting and discipleship.

- **Mental:** We also knew we wanted to focus the intellectual development of individuals through Christian education and training under our College program (Liberia International Christian College). Later we developed the *One Hour for Christ* Ministry, a scholarship assistance program for less-privileged children. We envisioned societal peace and harmony through transformed minds and leadership in communities.

- **Physical**: We knew that unless we had a vehicle for providing food for students and teaching them better farming techniques, they could not attend school. At the same time, we envisioned such a project being able to provide funding and technical assistance for local farmers in Liberia. That has since become a working farm called Hope Farm. We also were committed to supporting church construction and reconstruction projects, and sponsoring individuals in skill training programs and small business and micro-enterprise development for individuals.

- **The approach**: The cornerstone of all ULICAF's ministries was and is to work with Liberian nationals and American Christians across denominational boundaries to define and solve the problems that people and communities face by utilizing a broad array of strategies to ensure self-sufficiency. Through the past eight years, we have evolved into an effective international, faith-based organization. Several events and achievements have shaped the development of our organization and helped change the lives of hundreds of Liberians and communities we serve.

Working with church leaders in Liberia, we formulated the goal of ULICAF which is to respond to the four critical needs of the Liberian churches:

- Rebuilding the Liberian Church Infrastructure
- Church Renewal, Church Planting and Evangelism
- Training Pastors and Christian Leaders
- Education of Young Adults

Often, it is easier to look back and see God's plan than to understand it at the moment we are living it. In March 2002, Yah and I came to Indiana as homeless people in search of a temporary shelter. Grace Community Church became our home church. Here we found family-centered love and open-hearted kindness. Since then we have been actively involved in various small groups. We have found vision partners, and hundreds of core volunteers.

God led us to use our time wisely to register ULICAF as a non-for-profit 501(c) (3) organization which has allowed literally hundreds of American Christians to partner with us. And the Lord directed us to establish a core leadership team in Liberia to implement the college project!

ULICAF Board 2008

Chapter 15   Full Time Ministry At Last

The Lord providently closed the door to our return to Liberia in 2001. The city that we had planned to live in was totally overrun by Muslim rebels with more than half of its infrastructure destroyed and numerous people murdered in 2003.

Over these next couple of years I started praying and concentrating on reading the Bible with more thoughtfulness. I also read diverse Christian literature in order to broaden my perspective on the many ways God uses leaders of ministries. I learned much about God's sovereignty, love, and protection for His people. I began to examine what my own role might be in God's plan for Liberia. Eventually, after many visa delays and closed doors, I was developing an even deeper dependence on His provision for "everything" in life. I was painfully learning the importance of waiting on God for his timing.

Eventually, my prayers seemed to confirm I was ready for the next step in my ministry.

*　*　*　*　*　*　*　*　*　*　*　*

In 2005 I resigned from my job at John Marshall Middle School to devote myself full-time to ministry. Grace Community Church graciously consented to sponsor me and receive my support money because our organization did not yet have a 501(c)(3) status. The plan worked for about a year, but the initial leader who helped with the sponsorship resigned to pursue another ministry. I became desperate because I was told that I now needed to establish an alternate means of sponsorship and receiving support. I talked to my friend John Lieberman, the director of a Jewish evangelism ministry (Messianic Jewish Life - www.TheMessiah.org) and a former board member of ULICAF and we prayed about God's direction. John turned to me and said, "Sei, this may be the best thing that has happened to you because you need a way to broaden your support base and not depend on one church for your sole means of finances." He suggested that I write to all of my friends in America and let them know the situation so that they could pray for our needs and ministry.

I adamantly told John: "I don't believe I should raise support. Since my arrival in America, I had promised not to live on welfare." I shared how my first job in America was to mop floors and take out trash in our seminary building and offices from 5:30 a.m. to 7:30 a.m. before getting ready for my classes. I also mowed lawns, worked on blueberry farms, and cleaned churches to care for my family and to pay for my education. I wanted to express my appreciation for the blessings I had received already from so many friends and the great education I had received in this country. That is why I wanted to provide for my personal family and ministry needs through secular work.

When I got finished with this explanation, John said quietly: "I did not ask you to beg people, but just to ask people to pray for your ministry." So, I did what John suggested and sent out a prayer letter. I received some amazing answers. Friends wrote from various states and cities assuring us of their prayer and confirming the vision of our ministry.

I received a letter from Northwest Covenant Church in Mount Prospect with a check for a substantial amount to go toward support. The mission board chair explained that the funds were being sent from their own Liberia ministry account that had been set up by the Church a few years back. This was another confirmation of what God was planning for Liberia and that He wanted us to trust and obey Him alone, while giving others an opportunity to partner with us.

*   *   *   *   *   *   *   *   *   *   *   *

In 2006 we decided to host a Liberia Christian conference in Indianapolis. We also decided to expand our fellowship to include our American friends. If we were to build a college, we would need the help of as many Christians as possible that were excited about our vision.

During the past years, God has brought special people into our lives. As we were recruiting volunteers to help with the conference, Yah gave me the name of a certain lady to contact. She explained that this lady was a Bible study leader for Grace. She also led two women's Bible study groups at other churches. I scheduled a meeting with her. I explained our vision and she became passionate about what God was doing in our ministry. She then arranged for me to talk to the core leaders of the two study groups. We arranged for a meeting room at Grace and about ten to fifteen ladies came to hear me share my vision. During the meeting I asked her and her leaders if they could coordinate a banquet on our behalf to raise funds for the college project. She and her leaders accepted my request and began planning with me. At that same meeting she confirmed that "God was sending me like He did with Moses to serve my nation."

We held the conference banquet and raised over $27,000 for the college project. Since that time she has continued to give us generous financial support. She constantly reminds me that she has committed herself to praying for the immigration visa processing, and that God would watch over my family, and the ministry. (I need the appropriate immigration visa so that my children's visas are valid while I am in Liberia or traveling between the US and Liberia). At the time of this writing, one of my daughters has her own immigration visa and the other is beginning the process. One of the boys is not yet old enough so he might be able to be included with Yah and me, but our older son and daughter will have to go through it on their own.

Because of the many years I have lived in America, I have been able to help fellow Liberian refugees to find their way in this new American culture. The American and Liberian views are often quite different. For example, Americans and Liberians have different views of "community." To Liberians, communal interdependence and relationship are highly valued where in the United States individuality is emphasized.

When we decided to have the conference in the suburbs of Indianapolis, some of our Liberian supporters were concerned. We told them we were recruiting people to host them in their homes so they didn't have to stay in hotels. Most of these former refugees or students did not often have the chance to build friendships with people of different cultures. Most of the Liberians live in the bigger cities in the United States. I would often be asked, "What if we break something?" "What if we mess their home up?" Some of the Liberians were concerned that they wouldn't be able to relax with their suburban hosts. I reassured them that our American friends were not that different than us. I told them, "If your children break something in the house, just say 'I'm sorry.' "

The Bible describes true Christian fellowship where Jew and gentile, (cultures that remained separated by ethnicity and religion) became one "in Christ." Now, Liberian and American, black and white, rich and poor, can live in harmony and love one another. Jesus said, "By this they shall know they are my disciples, by their love one for another." Many Liberians, because of our ministry, have now been blessed as well as bringing a blessing to the Americans friends by living with them for a weekend.

Many Liberians and America have sacrificially given of their time and resources to help start LICC. Through Missions for Rural Africa I met Rev. A. Thomas Hill. He is the Senior Pastor at Healing Streams Worship Center in Indianapolis. He is a very gifted man of God with a special talent in leading worship. When we had our Liberian Conference at Grace, he provided the music and led the worship along with his congregation choir. From that beginning he became a partner with our organization.

Pastor Hill wrote, "Our ministry has already committed to support this worthwhile and much-needed mission in an area of the world that became a haven for many freed black slaves during the 1840s." He has supported us and introduced us to other African-American pastors and churches. Eastern Star Church made a contribution with a substantial amount toward the college's first year operational budget.

Prior to opening LICC, one of the key challenges was hiring qualified instructors and staff. We were also mindful of increasing tuition fees in the area where 75% of the people are unemployed. We knew that God would somehow provide a way for these students to attend the school when it opened. We would soon see how Christians would catch the vision and begin providing scholarships for these needy students.

Chapter 16   The Seedling: A School is Born

In 2004 we decided the time was right to purchase 20 acres of land near the city of Ganta to build the college. The cost was $13,500. These funds had primarily come from Liberian refugees since we had not yet begun to include Americans in our meetings.

We had chosen Ganta rather than the capital city, Monrovia, for several very practical reasons. Monrovia already had several colleges including a couple that were Christian. Ganta, however, was the second fastest growing commercial city. With an existing population of 68,000 it was expected to grow to over 100,000 within the next 10-12 years. They already had 19 high schools, but no college like we had planned, and thus our curriculum would be in demand by many graduating students. The cost of housing would be less in this area which obviously would enable more students to come from other cities.

Ganta was strategically located since the only major road leaving Monrovia to the south goes through Ganta. The city had electricity and bus lines and when the government starts to stabilize one day, Ganta would be high on their rebuilding priorities. It was located near other countries and in the region of various ethnicities.

Nimba County has a population of 468,88 population of Nimba County, and Ganta is heavily populated by the Mano and Gio ethnic groups. One could cross a river on one side of the city and enter the Republic of Guinea and meet several Mano ethnic communities. Also, one can cross from the north and enter the Ivory Coast to see several communities inhabited by the Gio ethnic groups. This relatively easy access to two countries would facilitate ministry opportunities for our students.

Ganta also has a mission hospital and several major banks and businesses. We had a good base from which to hire teachers from the surrounding high schools, use the services of missionaries from the hospital, and business people would be willing and able to teach part-time, possibly one course a semester. In this way we would not need to provide housing for them. We thought we could even get a part-time nurse for the school's clinic. We felt the Lord's leading as we prayed about the perfect location for the campus.

One of our partners in Liberia located a piece of property and immediately called me. With great excitement we purchased it and established an escrow account for the future construction work. Russ Schwartz and I had been working on the master plan and the design of the first classroom building.

When the war had subsided, the Lord indicated to us that it was time to create a core team of project planners. I knew of two pastors that served with the United Liberia Inland Church. It would be an opportunity to leave the war zone in Liberia and to have their faith strengthened. From 2005-2006 they were sponsored to Nairobi and received some practical training in Church planting from Nairobi Chapel, one of Grace Community Church's strategic partners.

One of the pastors, Anthony Gondoun, became the Project Manager. His role included purchasing all the materials and overseeing all phases of the construction. Although he had no construction background, he has been the brains behind the construction work of the building itself. He was so dedicated that in order to protect the materials from theft, he actually slept in the warehouse! He has supported us in every phase of the construction process even while continued his duties as a pastor.

*   *   *   *   *   *   *   *   *   *   *

We obviously have had many challenges along the way to starting LICC. One of the ongoing issues is raising funds. We started from nothing to build a campus for on-site living and needed a qualified faculty and staff. We moved forward trusting God to provide 100% for each new phase of the school. Many people that give to ministries see the immediate humanitarian crisis needs – AIDS, malnutrition, clean water, general health care, etc. and easily give to those works. They deserve funding and relief.

The problem with helping donors see the vision for education is that classroom training is not always seen as an *immediate* need for survival. ULICAF supports education because we are committed to building a sustainable future for poor communities in Liberia. Christ-centered education unlocks the potential of individuals by using their natural gifts and the training they receive. These students can and will go on to develop solutions to their community problems, especially in areas that were devastated by the civil war conflicts. We will invest in the individual's spiritual and intellectual growth. People affected by war and violence are often deeply traumatized, physically dislocated, and unable to continue their livelihoods. Education won't solve all of their problems, but it can help them adjust to the future and create new streams of income for themselves and their communities.

The United Nations estimates that there are about 800 million people in the world who cannot read or sign their own name. Most of these people live in Africa, South and East Asia, and the Arab states. Two thirds of them are women. Can you imagine how limited a person is if they can't sign their own name? Poverty remains a stronghold over the lives and future of whole communities of illiterate people. In the United States education has been one of the foundational pillars that has transformed the society from farmers to industrialists and currently into a technological/information society. Education has that same power for other communities and countries.

If the church and individuals will support the provision of a sound biblical education for underdeveloped communities, many of the relief needs will eventually take care of themselves. The people will have a foundation for solving more of their own problems. With God's grace they will be able to go on to help others. Almost everyone in ULICAF has this conviction that *literate people are more likely to read and understand the word of God, to create a sustainable living in poor communities, to make more informed decisions about their health, and to more actively support the next generation by helping their children attend school.* It is our challenge to communicate this message to the greater Church so that we might receive the support necessary to help our countrymen help themselves.

God gave us a vision to mobilize Liberian refugees and partner with American Christians to bring a renewed hope to the people of Liberia. I will never forget friends, churches, and organizations that have believed in us and in our vision. *We learned the important lesson in this process to enlist hundreds, preferably thousands, of believers to earnestly pray for us and the work.* Through my work with LICC, I understand clearly that people pray more regularly and earnestly for work they are involved in. When God leads me to someone, I without hesitation invite them to be our "vision partners." Our core values emphasize that we first and foremost look to God for the provision of our needs. If it is God's will, He will find a way to move His people to bless us and He will bless them in return.

Secondly, after prayer and petition to God, we then inform God's people of our needs and give them opportunities to get involved (II Cor. 8:12-15). Finally, we are extremely grateful for every gift we receive and diligently and prudently use it for the designated purpose. We know we are accountable to God and the people that give their support to help sustain LICC.

By working through these challenges, I am a changed man. God gave me a humble boldness to share with others the transforming power of a Christ-centered education.

Many of our challenges are more immediate and earthly. All we had was an undeveloped piece of land. We knew the obstacles to constructing even one building on that ground, but we kept the vision before us of 100 students eagerly learning God's Word and developing transferable job skills! We realized we could not do everything at once so we mapped out a strategy for everything from purchasing supplies, digging sand, hand-mixing cement, finding qualified faculty, writing the curriculum, and recruiting dedicated future students.

＊　＊　＊　＊　＊　＊　＊　＊　＊　＊　＊　＊

With a basic Master Plan and a blueprint for a first building, we were ready to think about actual construction. Here is what the Master Plan looked like at that point.

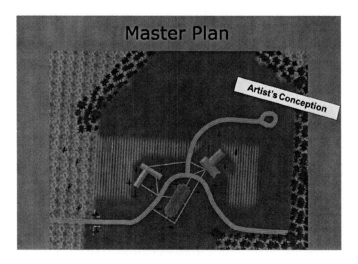

Original Master Plan

We realized that due to the lack of funds for an entire building, we would have to start with a first floor having a flat roof and build it in such a way that a second floor could be added to it. Our plan was to start small and grow. That would provide four classrooms, a business office, and a room in which to start a library. Large group instruction could be accomplished by opening a partition between two classrooms. A completion date was scheduled for Fall 2007.

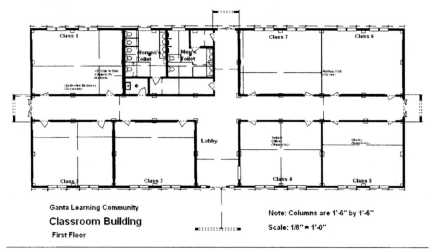

First Floor Layout

Within two years we plan to complete the second story with a hip roof. It would add seven to eight more classrooms and provide a workroom, lounge and three department offices. Our hope was to complete that by the end of 2008 or early in 2009.

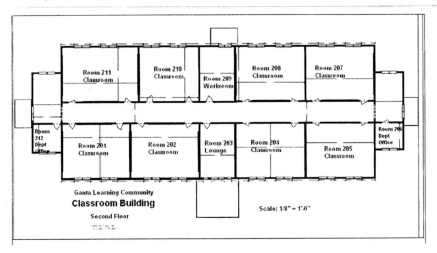

Second Floor Layout

As soon as this second story is completed, we could then think about building a separate dedicated library building which would also include a computer lab, some offices, and some classrooms, conference rooms, and research area filled with collections of books, CDs, DVDs. As funds were available we also could have an Internet café that would provide more interaction with the local community in Ganta.

I have mentioned the need for healthcare services and we plan for a clinic to initially meet the students' and faculty needs, but in showing Christian love, can be expanded to serve the greater Ganta community. It would be staffed by a physician and one or more nurses and have a mini-pharmacy. There is a possibility that clinic services could be expanded to the community as well. A small fee for such services could be used to support the services or the school.

* * * * * * * * * * * *

Simultaneously, we would have to create curriculum, hire staff, and figure out how the school would operate. We would also need to furnish the classrooms and offices, purchase office supplies including computers and copy machines, and purchase or create textbooks.

We created a 5 Phase Launch Plan to take place from August 2007 through August 2008 along with the construction outlined above:

Phase 1 – August 20 – October 20, 2007

- Develop Launch Plan
- Develop Mission, Vision, Core Values, and Beliefs for the school
- Develop Curriculum

Phase 2 – October 22, 2007 – January 11, 2008

- Appoint a Board of Trustees
- Develop Governance (Policies, Procedures, etc.)
- Develop Budget

Phase 3 – January 14 – March 28, 2008

- Hire Senior Staff
- Set Up Infrastructure
- Hire Teaching Faculty
- Establish External Relations

Phase 4 – March 31 – June 13, 2008

- Create Courses and Services
- Create School Catalog
- Market School to Recruit Students

Phase 5 – June 16 – August 31, 2008

- Matriculate Students
- Counsel and Register Students

ULICAF Board Meeting

Chapter 17   Challenges: Physical Campus

To guard against theft, since building supplies are hard to purchase and in great demand, we needed to construct a secure locked warehouse. We could not afford the risk of loss since it just takes so long to get supplies.

For example, in the United States, if you want cement for the foundation of a building, you can call a company and they deliver it pre-mixed at an agreed upon time. In Liberia, however, if you want cement, you have to personally drive your own truck to the river. If the river is not too high, *and* if there happens to be someone excavating the sand, you might be able to have this sand loaded into your truck. The men then must take the sand back to the site and unload it themselves. Next, you must find a store that has bags of concrete mix. Again you load them *yourself* and drive back and unload them. You often have to go to *several* stores, each in a different city, to find enough bags of cement to start the project. Then you take some empty 50-gallon drums (which you also have previously found and purchased) to the river, fill them with water, take them back and unload them. Now you have the basic cement ingredients to *hand*-mix in a wheelbarrow (which you had previously purchased). This is a laborious process since you have to use one wheelbarrow load at a time to pour the walls. Imagine what it would be like and how long it would take to build even a modest sized church building in the United States by this procedure!

We faced additional building challenges. Before we began, we needed to prepare the ground and made sure that it was level before pouring the foundation. We also needed wood concrete forms created for the walls. We needed many workers, both men and women, to mix all of the cement and roll the heavy wheelbarrows up inclined planks to pour it into the walls.

My good friend, Lee Wuanti, a fellow Liberian now living in Noblesville, Indiana was a former high school teacher and has a heart to be available to do whatever the Lord calls him to do so that the people of Liberia can benefit both spiritually and materially. When I asked him to represent ULICAF in Liberia to lay the foundation for the first building of the college, he and his wife Narko were excited that the Lord could use them to help facilitate the laying of the foundation, a dream come true.

Lee sent out a prayer letter (from which the quotes were taken) which outlined his responsibilities. He would:

- Build relationships with local Christians and encourage them in their walk with God

- Meet with local Christian leaders and encourage them to support the Bible College both financially and prayerfully

- Personally assist with the preparation of the site and the laying of the foundation

Lee raised his own support and worked tirelessly laying the foundation April 5 through May 5, 2006.

Chris Royston, a Grace Community Church attendee, accepted our invitation to go on a short-term mission trip to Liberia from the end of September until the end of December of 2006. Chris used his construction background and training to become the construction supervisor to help get the building up and ready for students. He willingly left his wife and young son and his job for three months to "fulfill the Lord's call on his life."

Upon the completion of the foundation work, we contracted with a local construction group to build the first floor of the first classroom building. At one point the construction task slowed down considerably. Our local contractor had demanded compensation much higher than his initial estimate and well beyond our itemized budget. We simply did not have the money. We faced the unpleasant task of going back to our partners to ask for more money. These wonderful partners had already helped us so much.

Using a Ramp to Transport Cement

I prayed over this issue. Shortly afterwards, I received an invitation to speak at a Lamplighter men's retreat sponsored by Grace Community Church. I spoke to the men on the theme, "Grace: the Radiance of God's Love." Afterwards, God began a new healing process in my life concerning the repeated theme of God's grace and the Holy Spirit's leading me into challenges wherein I have to trust God for "everything" in my life. God answered many of my prayers. Precious brothers and sisters, there is something amazing about God's grace!

In our particular situation God intervened on our behalf and we were able to replace the labor group with an excellent hard-working group of Christian workers that charged us 60% less per hour! The new contractor agreed to provide, at these same rates, even additional services which included raising the walls, plumbing, installing electrical work, plastering, and laying the floor tiles. When they were finished, we would only need to paint and furnish the building.

We completed the construction of the first classroom building and dedicated it on June 14, 2008. Our goal was to commence operation in the fall of 2008 by accepting as many as one hundred students in the first year.

LICC Building at Dedication

Due to delays in processing government paperwork, problems getting textbooks, and not having all teaching staff on site, our start date was delayed to March 2, 2009.

The Pre-calculus class and Systematic Theology class started simultaneously at 4:00 pm. Counselor Mewaseh Paye-bayee, a veteran educator who taught at Liberia University and now owns a law firm in Ganta, challenged and encouraged the anxious and eager students in his class to try their best to become masters over Mathematics. In the Systematic Theology class, Rev. James Lablah introduced the students to Theology, its systematic order and how it relates to other major theologies of the Bible. The two classes combined at 7:00 pm to become a Christian Ethics class under Rev. Sampson Nyanti. Christian Ethics is one of the general required courses.

Fifty students attended orientation, but on the first day of classes we had a total attendance of 64 men and women, which increased to 82 by the second day! These excited college students have no textbooks and so, for now, they depend on handouts.

LICC First Students

Below is the press release from that event:

FOR IMMEDIATE RELEASE

Dr. Sei Buor, President
Liberia International Christian College
16840 Maraschino Dr.
Noblesville, IN 46062
317.773.9751
www.LiberiaInternationalCC.org
www.ULICAF.org
fsbuor1@gmail.com

Liberia International Christian College Welcomes First Students

Indianapolis, IN – March 9, 2009 – Sixty-four students were welcomed to orientation at Liberia International Christian College in Ganta City, Nimba County, Liberia, on March 2, 2009. By Friday afternoon, the three classes of this term had an attendance of 82 students, most of whom must walk or bicycle several miles to school. This unique college is believed to be the first indigenous college in Liberia, West Africa. While this inaugural class will major in either business or ministry, there will be other majors, a trade school and a self-supporting farm also.

LICC has been started by ULICAF, the United Liberia Inland Church Associates & Friends, which is comprised mainly of Liberians who were displaced by 14+ years of civil war and destruction. ULICAF was founded in 2000 to provide fellowship and encouragement to refugees resettled in the United States and to provide spiritual and humanitarian support for the nation of Liberia. While working two or three jobs to support their families, Liberian refugees began to give to ULICAF with the vision of starting a college in Liberia to educate future leaders in business, government, medical fields, education, ministry, and agriculture.

Dr. Sei Buor has coordinated all efforts of financial support, building, hiring staff and faculty, and setting the structure and direction of the college from his office near Indianapolis, Indiana. Because Dr. Buor is originally from Nimba County, Liberia, (population: 468,000) and he spent many years attempting to get a good education in Liberia, he knows the problems and needs of the country. According to Dr. Buor, "Education changed my life. Getting an education has allowed me to live a life I would never have experienced had I remained a farmer in my village. . . . I have had the chance to touch the lives of so many people."

For more information: Dr. Sei Buor
317.773.9751 or fsbuor1@gmail.com

\# \# \#

*   *   *   *   *   *   *   *   *   *   *   *

Initially, we had started getting books for a seminary, and while this was important for theology classes, we still needed textbooks and library books for other subjects. We needed (and still need) books for English and business courses. A single new textbook can cost as much as $40-$75 in the United States. A Liberian student struggles to afford that much for tuition so buying textbooks for four or five classes is out of the question. We are using a variety of options for textbooks such as a rental plan to leverage the cost of a book over several semesters for some books or purchasing a few copies and putting them "on reserve" in the library.

We faced utility challenges, especially the need for electricity. We did have water from our own well, but we had no electricity since there was no electricity available for the city itself. We needed a large generator which is a "big ticket item" to us and costs around $20,000. This would include enough power for the computer equipment/room to both service the computers and protect them from damage by surges and power outages.

We were able to locate a company in Florida that could provide the right size and type of generator for less than $20,000; however, the shipping costs were very expensive. Therefore, we began looking for other companies that could supply us a generator in Liberia. When we researched generators we were amazed that it cost less than half of what we expected to pay. In this way, the Lord provided a main generator and we even had funds to buy a back-up generator!

Generator and Back-up

Generator Housing

Throughout the founding of LICC, as we face each new challenge, we truly have had to rely on Him. It is true we have experienced enough of God's blessings to have faith in His provision. Our faith is growing day by day. But, that does not mean we know how or when He will provide. And, God's timing is sometimes not ours.

We have come a long way, but we know the journey is still in its infancy stages. Even as we look back on the past challenges, we know there will be trials to test our faith in God's sufficiency and provision. I thank God for all those people He has put in our path to be His hands and feet.

Chapter 18   Confirmations: Faculty and Staff

A Christian college obviously needs a campus with adequate buildings; a school, however, must have qualified Christian dedicated teachers even more. The Lord has blessed us with a small but godly faculty and staff for the college. The following stories will introduce you to a few of them, including three of our full-time staff. You will soon agree that each one was hand-picked and sent by God.

One of our faithful staff members is Christian Zarweah, a man in his early forties. I became acquainted with Christian when I went to a meeting of Liberian Refugees in Minnesota. We began talking about people of integrity. The woman that led the Minnesota fellowship said she knew someone that had those qualities. She told us about the man that had been her pastor in their refugee camp in Liberia.

I called Christian and introduced myself. Christian said, "Yes, I may not know you personally, but I know all about you. I know about your preaching and teaching, Dr. Buor." So I asked him to help us. We were right in the middle of the construction project of our guesthouse. We sent him $10,000 to complete the guesthouse and also told him that the deadline was less than two months away! Additionally, we told him he must document exactly how the money was spent, including all receipts. He said that he could do it.

Christian completed the project on time and within our budget! This demonstrated to me not only his integrity, but also his diligence in planning and finishing projects. Christian also had a Master's Degree in Christian Education from the Assembly of God Graduate school of Theology in Lome, Togo. Since Christian has shown us his faithfulness, we decided to make him our team leader in Ganta and appointed him as Vice President for the school.

The next person God sent out way was Judy Thurman from Asheville, North Carolina. She had come to Liberia on a one-year contract to work with a mission group. She had a military background and was a strong leader. Just as she nearing the end of her contract and was ready to return home, she met with Christian Zarweah. When he told her the story of the school and the need for teachers, she decided to visit our campus.

Judy told Christian, "If you want me to come and teach, please have your President give me a call." Well, that was not going to be a problem. We sent her some information and I contacted Judy. She told me, "Teaching is my passion." She was willing to come and teach, but I told her, "Judy, we can't afford to pay you."

Judy responded, "I don't need a salary. I worked for the U.S. Navy for 40 years. Also, I am a member of a church and will trust God for my support; if I fall short, the pastors and congregation will support me if necessary."

I told Judy, "I need you to come to Indiana so we can talk one-on-one." Judy agreed. So, on June 26th, 2008, Judy came to Indianapolis. We had several subsequent meetings. She met with both the Liberian group and our American friends and everyone agreed that Judy was a good fit for our campus.

Judy signed a commitment for three to five years and left a copy with us. On July 8th she took a plane to Liberia. Today, Judy is the chairlady for our English Department and Director of Admissions and Scholarships. She is also working on setting up the library.

Judy related to me that for two years, while enjoying retirement, God impressed on her the need to go to the mission field and teach. In Judy's words: "I went to Liberia and worked for one year with a faith-based agency, primarily in Nimba County. During that year, God opened doors for me to teach English which I did for a junior college and a seminary. Then, I heard about LICC and their need for English instructors."

Another one of our faithful staff is Lawrenso Korquoi. Lawrenso is my nephew. I became involved in Lawrenso's life during the time I was in Bible College. Lawrenso was one or two years old at the time and was very ill with measles. He was almost dying. You could see that from the condition of his tongue.

His father and mother had brought him to see a witch doctor to find out if his illness was the result of a curse. I asked my sister and brother-in-law if I could take him to a hospital. But, they said, "No, the witch doctor said that it was a spell from another witch doctor." This was ridiculous! I grabbed Lawrenso and took him to a hospital near my college. It was 1:00 a.m. in the morning and I found a nurse on duty that quickly came to my aid and rushed Lawrenso into a room to begin preparing him for treatment. I waited and prayed outside the room and by God's grace Lawrenso survived. The health care worker said, "If you hadn't gotten him to a hospital, he surely would have died." Since that day, Lawrenso has been like a son to me.

During the civil war, he went to high school. His father died of illness during the war and so Yah and I decided to send him to the AME Zion University in Liberia. He studied business management and learned other computer skills that led me to appoint him as our business manager. He writes our reports which go to both Grace Community Church and our Board.

Rev. Sampson Nyanti who taught our first Christian Ethics class will be the instructor for a variety of courses that lead to a Bachelor's Degree in Christian Education and Pastoral Studies. Rev. Sampson is the Superintendent of the Ganta United Methodist Mission, Associate Pastor of the Miller McAllister United Methodist Church, and the District Evangelist responsible for church planting and evangelism. His Bachelor of Arts is from African Bible College and his Master of Divinity in Pastoral Studies is from JOS ECWA Theological Seminary in Nigeria.

Rev. Nyanti confirms that he has "been in the business of educating Liberians for a long time." He was my replacement at Saclepea Inland Mission School and the church in 1988.

Part of his job is to "train young Liberians in the areas of vocational trade so that they can develop marketable skills." Since the five-year plan includes the establishment of a trade school, his expertise will be invaluable. For these reasons, Christian felt he was a good fit for LICC and asked him to become a part of the teaching staff. Interestingly, LICC's secretary was trained by Sampson.

We know that Sampson has personal academic goals to get a PhD. We will miss him as he works on his doctorate, but we hope he will return to us well-equipped to enable us to broaden and develop further our programs.

Individualized Help from Professor

Large Group Instruction

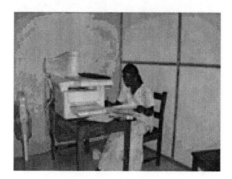

Student at ComputerStudying Between Classes

Taking Notes

Classes are Large and Well Attended

Chapter 19   Next Steps

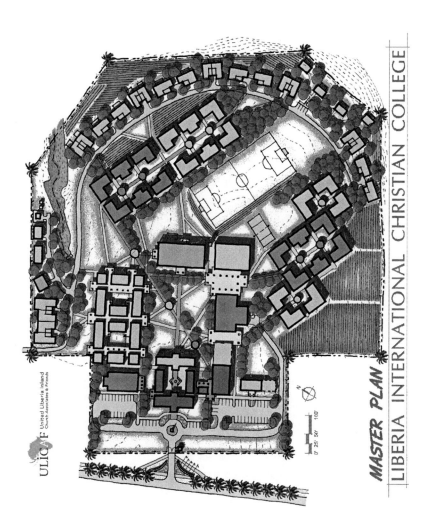

The New Master Plan

Phase 1 is finished and phase 2 of the construction is starting.

Where are we in the phases of starting the college? We have our first class, but we are working hard to stay one step ahead of the students as we create the curriculum and hire faculty to teach them next year. That will continue for several years as we introduce more curriculum and more courses in the curriculum.

Physical Facilities:

We have worked diligently with our Board to create a long-term Master Plan (as seen on the previous page) that includes many more pieces than our original Master Plan. One of our partners, Margaret Beach and her family made a generous financial gift enabling us to build a water tower in honor of their late sister Eleanor May Cermark.

The water tower is the main source of supply to the entire campus, but we are still striving to find a means for water purification to provide clean drinking water to the water fountains on campus.

Our goals by the end of 2010 are to:

- complete construction of the second floor to add 7 more classrooms and offices, and furnish those rooms,
- supply textbooks to a growing student body and faculty,
- increase the collections of the library, to purchase needed office supplies and adequate computers,
- install outdoor lighting and landscaping (trees, plants)
- create visible signage on the road,
- provide a purified water system throughout the campus.

Our goal by 2015 is

- to have a library building finished and equipped and a clinic built and equipped. That will include some classrooms/conference rooms, a computer lab, research areas, and a bookstore. This facility would also provide Internet service for the campus and perhaps to the community. A clinic building may or may not provide service to the area as well as the school.

Beyond 2015 we would be prepared to start trades classes and construct a building for teaching trades.

Faculty and Staff:

The goals by the end of 2010 are:

* ♣ Increase the number of professors in theology, business, and education;

* ♣ Add an administrator to work with Christian;

* ♣ Confirm an Academic Dean and a Dean of Students;

* ♣ Provide professional seminars for the development of staff on a regular basis; and

* ♣ Provide well-developed job description for each teaching position.

* ♣ By 2010 our faculty would include enough full-time and part-time instructors (either on site or planning to come) to teach the courses needed for the business degree and the pastoral studies degree.

* ♣ By 2015 we will have in place the system of professional development to encourage lecturers to get a master's (or doctorate) degree either online or by going to a nearby university. All the instructors needed for the business degree and the Christian education and pastoral studies degrees would be in place so that our first graduating class would be able to graduate. Other degree programs would be started and their instructors would be identified and in the process of being on campus when needed.

Students:

The short-term goals for students include

- Increasing the student body as classrooms and teaching staff allow;

- Developing part-time student program as separate from full-time student programs;

- Increasing scholarship and grant funding for students.

Longer-term goals for students would be:

- transportation (cars, vans) that would be available to students and staff for a small fee

- Develop internship plan for graduates with Associate's or Bachelor's degrees in churches, parachurch organizations, business, and government. The Bachelor's degrees in Pastoral Studies, Christian Education, and Business would be fully implemented. Other majors would be started.

- Beyond 2015, there are plans for a functional agricultural farm to teach better farming practices and to produce fruits and vegetables for the school and for sale.

The Big Strategic Plan:

In the short term,

- We need excellent security for the campus. That includes computer security (data security) and building security to provide for the safety of students and faculty.

- We also need drinking water that is safe.

- We will have ongoing needs of communication to explain the growth of the school to our constituents.

- We will begin the process of setting up scholarships for students and endowments for paying instructors.

♣ We will explore various means of support, especially as they strengthen our relationships with our community or with our supporters.

By 2015 we must raise a steady means of support through grants, planned giving, and endowments. We need to create other forms of support such as services, partnerships and networks. Fund raising will be a large piece of future strategic plans.

What will the student body look like?

The student body of Liberia International Christian College will be comprised of responsible men and women in their late 20s through early 40s who are high school graduates. They would primarily be business people, pastors or government leaders, but many would not have a career as yet. All would feel called by the Lord to a particular job or area of service.

Younger students would be those wanting to start business or wanting to prepare for ministry. Young adults who are doing small business in the city would enroll to grow their businesses, so evening classes will be in demand to give them fresh ideas.

Of necessity, most students will continue to be from within 10 miles of Ganta. However, many citizens of Ganta have fled from villages and farms to find safety and/to make a living. They may take their new skills back to their farms and villages.

The students will be encouraged to set a high standard of ethics as well as model professional behavior and biblical values in their words and behavior. They will also be mentored by appropriate faculty members and will, in turn, mentor others throughout their lives. They will be adept at research but will also be experienced with applying their faith in everyday situations and sharing their faith with those in their sphere of influence. They will continue to seek to improve themselves and their communities. They will take with them a deep appreciation for God-given talents and skills and a deep-seated desire to use their skills for the furthering of God's kingdom.

Chapter 20   Vision for the Future

At times, it is easy to be overwhelmed by the day-to-day tasks of starting a school and get myopic, and thereby lose sight of the overall vision. The long-term vision is what enables us to get through present challenges. The first question we have to keep in mind is, "Why are we doing this?"

I have several answers. First of all, in the wake of years of civil unrest and a poor economy, our youth have lost faith. It's not difficult to see how our young people are easily broken by years of poverty, guerilla warfare, death and destruction. One of our goals is to model a servant leadership by sharing that we really care about their problems. We do this by giving them opportunity in education, job skills and training that is relevant to the practical need of the community. The education we impart will not just be facts or professional skills. Our goal is to go beyond that. We want to impact the student's character. We hope to inspire a vision for what God can do in them if they build their lives on Christian values.

Second, and very important, because our nation has sixteen different major ethnic groups in fifteen different counties, we will have student representatives from all over the country. That way, *our students can have a big impact when they graduate, return to their home county, transform their community, and our nation.*

Third, I imagine one day traveling throughout Liberia and seeing grade schools, high schools, trade schools, even colleges and universities. I envision that most Liberian children will be offered the opportunity to attend a grade school to learn to read, write, and perform basic arithmetic. Those children will learn for the first time the true history of their country including the brutal facts of our civil war. Then, hopefully, they won't repeat the worst parts of our history. I see neighborhood schools and communities close to where the students live. I see so many schools that few students have to walk 20 miles, or even 10 miles, to school each day. I see schools with trained teachers. And, yes, our hope is that some of those teachers will have been trained at our college. Our hope is that many teachers who wouldn't otherwise have been able to receive an education themselves actually will have received one because of LICC.

I envision medical hospitals and clinics. I can see one day the average Liberian having a chance to visit a medical doctor or trained nurse when necessary. I imagine enough medical clinics that patients can be treated in their own area, and not have to travel long distances. Our hope is that some of them will have received their initial undergraduate training by attending LICC.

I imagine government leaders who are not only trained in modern business and administrative techniques, but also have had their Christian values sharpened at LICC. They will know the difference between light and darkness, between right and wrong, and will have seen faith in action. They will have been taught that a government position is a position of trust, and that God wants them to be faithful stewards of their positions.

We lost many church leaders during the civil war. Now, we need new leaders to arise. To help meet this need, I see pastors who receive their training at LICC. I see them going back to their communities to share their faith like I did. I imagine many people coming to a faith in Jesus, and I foresee that faith maturing under the leadership of pastors, some of whom were trained at LICC.

As the second part of the long-term vision, we hope that *all of Liberia* can see this school as an example of what can be done with God's help. And that LICC will inspire other colleges to come into existence. It would not hurt my feelings if people see what we have done, want to do it themselves, and end up doing even more than we have done! In fact, I would love to see LICC become a template that extends to all of West Africa and, in particular, our neighboring countries.

We hope to be a template for more than just how to start a college. When Christ asks us to redeem the world and to advance His Kingdom, what does this mean for a small, developing African country which is in the process of recovering from a civil war?

When Jesus walked this earth He didn't just *talk about* spiritual truths. He met people's spiritual and physical needs. He healed the sick, fed the hungry, and "walked with" his followers in community.

He was redeeming individual lives which impacted the life of the whole community by both preaching and *acting out* the good news. After His resurrection he preached to his disciples, but he also made breakfast for them as they came in from fishing one morning.

Similarly, education is only one part of community and national redemption. Other related facets are health care, economic development, safe water, disease prevention, technology, and developing the community infrastructure such as roads, communication networks, water, and sewage, etc. A vision for an education is a first and necessary step. "Without vision, the people perish." Without vision there is no redemption and no sustainable community of faith. Is all of the above too much to ask? Is such a vision "unrealistic?" Not for our God!

The mission of LICC is a global collective effort. God has brought Americans and refugees together. I hope this can be a model for other areas. We want to encourage people to get together at the grassroots level. We want to encourage them to work together to alleviate poverty, illiteracy, and address health concerns; to bring peace between divergent cultures.

Other leaders may not be inspired to build a college, but they can be part of the vision of redeeming of peoples, cultures and the world for the Kingdom of God by their generous support.

Finally, we want LICC to be a *sign for our people of what God can do*. We want to establish a memorial beacon. What do I mean by that? In the Book of Joshua, when the children of Israel crossed over into the Promised Land, one of the things they did was to create a pile of stones as a memorial and witness to what Yahweh had done.

When the people of God crossed into the land that God has promised, they were crossing a barrier, the Jordan River. God was with them and He parted the river. They walked on dry land and entered their Promised Land. So, at God's direction, they built a pillar of stones. Our hope is that LICC will become a memorial to God's faithfulness to a fragile people who had no means of achieving God's plan. In both cases it is God doing the working! And just like the pillar of stone, LICC stands as a pillar pointing to the powerful hand of God and exhorting us to always revere the awe of His greatness.

We want future generations to know that LICC represented a vision so strong that it empowered people without resources to build such a school. We hope that such a memorial will enable them to see God's faithfulness, much as the pillar of stones reminded the Israelites of God's faithfulness.

Some of the people who will hear of our story will establish ministries that witness to God's faithfulness in their lives and to the community. How will the impact of this memorial unfold? What will those who are affected do in response? We do not know, but can hope. We can hope that our little school will act like a "Jordan River event" in the lives of our brothers and sisters. Imagine what future "Promised Land events" can become a reality as we humbly follow God's leading in His redeeming all of life to the Kingdom of Christ.

Our vision is to see LICC grow into a major Christian *University*. When that day comes, I want to make sure that we never forget our humbled beginnings. We have many more obstacles to face. May we always acknowledge along the way the ONE for whom the college exists. It was established to bring honor to God and to raise up and educate His leaders. These men and women will be called to lead a once broken impoverished and devastated war-torn nation into a new age of prosperity grounded in Christian values. How this will exactly unfold in the years ahead, I don't know. We want to "run well the course God set before us." We accept Jesus' words as our ongoing marching orders:

"With man this is impossible, but not with God; all things are possible with God." (Mark 10:27 – NIV)   and "Everything is possible for him who believes." (Mark 9:23 - NIV)

Your Part in God's Education Plan for Liberia

I hope that as you have read this story, you have allowed God to stir your heart. Only our Great God could, in His Omniscience and Omnipotence, direct the events of my life and formally establish LICC and bring about the training that we are already offering. If you sense an excitement, anticipation, concern and amazement at what God has done already, then join us.

Please look through this chapter and let God speak to you. There are many ways in which you can become involved, some of which are probably unknown to me. You may have read about some of the needs we perceive we will have, but you may have skills or training in an area that was not mentioned. We may not even know what our needs will include as we expand and offer more classes and services to our students. Whatever your interest, skills, and abilities are, please contact us so that we can match you to an opportunity with our ministry.

Our short-term needs are:

- *Construction Supervisor.* The ideal candidate would be able to devote 3-6 months to a project and would work in Liberia.

- *Computer Specialist.* The ideal candidate would spend one month to one year setting up computers and networks and even teaching students to use the computers.

- *Library Specialist.* This is a short-term mission position to help with set up and ongoing cataloging of books and materials. This person must have a degree in media. This might include providing training to staff.

- *School Administrator.* This would be a short-term mission position to create a database and put records in order. He or she would also create job descriptions and do many other tasks to prepare the school to run smoothly for the long term. (Could be an administrative assistant from a school.)

<u>Our long-term needs are:</u>

- ***Business Professors***. These people would teach college level business courses for a semester, a year, or multiple semesters. Experience teaching business courses at the college level is desired.

- ***Biblical Languages Professor***. This person would teach Greek or Hebrew for one or more semesters.

- Various ***other professors*** for varying lengths of time. We will be needing instructors for courses in theology, Christian education, preaching, evangelism, etc.

<u>Our needs in the United States are:</u>

- ***Newsletter editor and writers***. This job is based in the US. The person would work on bi-monthly newsletters.

- ***Special Scholarships Coordinator***. This US-based person would match students with funding needs to individuals or organizations that desire to sponsor a student.

- ***Fund Developer***. This person could be located anywhere, but must work to find grants and create various means for funding the school and the students. This person would be familiar with various types of funding, networking, and developing partnerships.

- ***Special Events Coordinator***. This is a US-based job planning (and helping to host) dinners, home fellowships, and other types of activities.

- ***Endowment and Trust officer***. This person would be US-based and would help with setting up trusts and endowments to benefit the school.

- ***Vision Partners***. These are people who share in our vision, pursue our mission, and give regularly to it. *Everyone is qualified to be a Vision Partner, so please join us in this capacity!*

<u>Our needs for physical items to be purchased or donated and shipped to Liberia are:</u>

- ***Textbooks*** for classes, books for the library (all types)
- ***Supplies*** for students and professors – office supplies, fans, various items.
- ***Classroom supplies*** – chairs and desks
- ***Computers, printers, copy machines*** - also paper and printer cartridges
- ***Furniture*** – for offices and administrative areas, for classrooms, for lounges for students and for faculty and later for dormitories and guest houses

See our web site at <u>http://www.ulicaf.org/get_involved.php</u> for a current list of needs.

We have opportunities for short-term mission trips to Liberia and to LICC. We provide accommodations and meals at reasonable costs. Liberia has wonderful fresh fruits and vegetables. We also plan activities for you to help you become better acquainted with the culture and know some of the people personally. If you prefer to stay with a family, we can arrange that. It is called a ***Taste of the Culture***. We hope that if you take a mission trip to Liberia, you will grow spiritually as well as work hard and have fun.

For more information about opportunities to become involved with Liberia International Christian College, contact:

Dr. Sei Buor
317.773.9751
<u>fsbuor1@gmail.com</u>
ULICAF
P. O. Box 1158
Carmel IN 46082

Dr. Buor would also be interested in speaking to your Bible study group, church group or any other group about ULICAF or LICC.

There are always financial needs for the school and for individuals. Donations are tax-deductible. To give a one-time gift or to start giving on a monthly basis or to endow a scholarship fund, please contact:

Ruth Schwartz
317.566.8390
ruths@gracecc.org
ULICAF
P. O. Box 1158
Carmel IN 46082

Mrs. Schwartz is very knowledgeable about ULICAF and LICC and can answer a variety of questions. However, if neither Dr. Buor nor Mrs. Schwartz is available, please feel free to contact the President of the Board of ULICAF:

Mr. Karney Dunah
603.461.1314
kdunah@svmservices.com
1418 Green Oak Trail
Aurora, IL 60505

United Liberian Inland Church Association and Friends (ULICAF)

www.ulicaf.org
ULICAF
P.O. Box 1158
Carmel, IN 46082
Phone: 317.773.9751
Executive Director: Sei Buor, Ph.D.
Donations are tax-deductible.
Contact: Dr. Sei Buor at 317.417.3111 or fsbuor1@gmail.com.

Liberian International Christian College

www.liberiainternationalcc.org
Liberia International Christian College
Ganta City, Nimba County
Republic of Liberia
Phone: 011-231-6-640-118
Contact: Russ and Ruth Schwartz at 317.566.8390 or ruths@
gracecc.org
Contact in Liberia: Christian Zarweah, Executive Vice President of
LICC at 011-231-6-640-118 or christianzarweah2000@yahoo.fr

Photos

Benjamin's High School Graduation

Marsha Cleon- our spiritual daughter

Sei, Deizie, Yah, Ben, and Saye

Yah and Sei

The Buor Family Today

Tonzia's Graduation from Anderson University

About the Author

Sei Buor is the executive director of ULICAF in Noblesville, Indiana, and President of Liberia International Christian College. From an early age Sei was committed to pursuing an education. He continued that commitment after his life-changing acceptance of Jesus Christ as his Lord and Savior. This eventually led him to America to study at Western Theological Seminary in Holland, Michigan (Th.M in Theology) and Loyola University in Chicago for a PhD in Educational Leadership and Policy Studies.

This is the story of Sei's early life in rural Liberia, his pursuit of education in spite of impossible odds, his development as a Christian leader, and his inspiration to lead his fellow refugees in a mission of love for Liberia.

If you would like to contact Dr. Buor for speaking engagements, please use the following:

Dr. Sei Buor
fsbuor1@gmail.com
ULICAF
P. O. Box 1158
Carmel IN 46082
www.ULICAF.org
www.Liberiainternationalcc.org

LaVergne, TN USA
29 October 2009
162488LV00002B/2/P